A YEAR
WITHOUT
FEAR

L. HARRY SEXTON

ISBN 978-1-63814-457-1 (Paperback)
ISBN 978-1-63814-458-8 (Digital)

Covenant Books, Inc.
11661 Hwy 707
Murrells Inlet, SC 29576
www.covenantbooks.com

To Cindy (my wife), Patty (mother-in-law), and Milly (mother).
They are the three women in my life who have each demonstrated,
at critical times in their lives, a level of fearlessness
that is beyond comprehension.

Introduction

I was raised going to church. Pretty much if the doors were open, my family was there. The week started with Sunday morning and Sunday evening service. Then there were the Wednesday evening club meetings and Bible study and finally any special youth events on Friday nights or Saturday that almost always included some sort of Bible message, even if it was a brief one. So I figured that I have spent somewhere over twelve thousand hours over the last sixty-plus years being involved in some sort of organized Bible instruction, which did not include my own personal study time as I have prepared Sunday school lessons and the occasional sermon. This should have braced me to withstand anything that this world and Satan threw at me, and yet fear, in all its various incarnations, continually seemed to be just at the edge of my peripheral vision, trying to get me to at best just stop and hunker down and try to withstand whatever was coming at me or at worst to retreat, to admit some level of defeat, and to give up the ground that I had already walked past in the name of some sort of self-preservation.

I think that with age, various forms of fear become more acute due to experience. You have gone through situations or have been close to others who have and so you develop a heightened sense of what could go wrong, usually in the physical realm. This, of course, stands in stark contrast to the days of your youth when you de facto believed, and lived like, nothing could ever harm you. And yet, as I have raised my five children, I have observed that there are fears that tend to be really heightened during those junior high, high school, and early college years. Fears like failure, rejection, criticism, change, gossip, embarrassment, inadequacy, disappointment, and being disappointing seem to be at an all-time high. Now that, of course, is not to say that those fears do not follow us into adulthood; they do and can be quite debilitating. But in my experience at least is that they often tend to be more powerful in the younger years. Now combine all that with those thousands of hours of looking into God's Word and seeing over and over again that I should not be afraid, and I had to stop and really look at why fear continued to play such a dominant role in my life. What had I missed? What did I need to do differently so that I could be that fearless person that I should be?

Now before I go on much further, I do not think that my friends and family would think that I live my life with a fear battle going on. For most of my twenty-seven years with the Phoenix Police department, I was a street cop working second shifts, which statistics will bear out are the most dangerous hours to be in law enforcement. And for the most part, I loved every minute of it. Less than a year into my career, I was faced with a deadly situation and had to respond with deadly force at a distance of about two feet. If you talk to most self-defense instructors, they will probably tell you that if a bad guy with a large carving knife gets that close to you with the intent to harm you, they got way too close. And yet that experience only served to hone my awareness and to cause me to rely on the training and instruction that I had received at the police academy.

I have to admit that I do harbor one particular fear that my family has used to their continual amusement, which is spiders. My kids would joke that their dad will go into a bar full of fighting bikers with backup five minutes out with no problem. But if he sees one little grass spider coming off the bill of his ball cap, he will wreck the car, trying to get away from it. This spider issue, of course, meant that I would find small fake spiders, which had been judicially placed, so that I would find them when I least expected it. Nothing like living in a house of practical jokers when they know you have a weak spot! But the problem became that as I experienced more and more potential situations that could have left me or one of my fellow officers dead or gravely wounded, I began to have a better sense of what I should be concerned about. My peripheral vision had widened a bit into the shadow area of possibilities. Then one by one, my children started getting their driver's license and going out into the world, and

6

those shadow possibilities combined with my experiences in dealing with the mayhem of life allowed those possibilities to take on the appearance of form and substance. As a result, I began to be afraid.

As I started to grapple with those various fears, I realized that what it really came down to was an issue of control. Take those nasty, ugly, creepy (and really, God, did we need them?) spiders. They have their own little spider mind, and I cannot control what they do. Plus, having been raised in an area where black widow spiders are prevalent, I know that some types of spiders can be downright dangerous. So while there is a good reason not to mess with them and there are plenty of products on the market to deal with them, I cannot control them so the result is a form of fear. The same is true with a lot, if not most, other fears. It comes down to a situation, person, or thing that you cannot control to which you perceive yourself to be vulnerable in some way. Then the self-preservation part of you kicks in, and you experience what is called the fight-or-flight syndrome, and you are off to either the physical, mental, or emotional races. See you when you get back; that is, if you get back. Then I took another look at what the Bible had to say about fear and being afraid. And it says over and over again not to do it and often employs the language of command structure, so it really is not an option. Next, I looked at the life of Jesus Himself. He had some concerns since He was temporarily housed in a human body, but He walked right into what He already knew was going to be horribly painful, degrading, and lonely. This was the ultimate three-way attack on the body, soul, and spirit.

I looked at other heroes of the Bible who appeared to have the same kind of fearlessness that Jesus had: Paul, Stephen, and Peter in the New Testament. Then Daniel, Shadrach, Meshach, and Abednego in the Old Testament, just to name a few. So I had to determine, Was this something special that I could only read about or was this something that every Christian could experience? If it was the latter, then I knew that Scripture would weigh in on it. I began my research by reading and then copying and pasting every verse in the Bible that simply used the words *fear* in some form or the word *afraid*. That came up to a whopping 671 verses! So when a word or concept shows up that often, there is something to be learned there.

I followed that up by reading them over and over and numbering those that had a particular concept as opposed to those verses that just used the term in a more general way. Finally, I began to try to group them into similar concepts, which led me to put all this down into written form so that I could share it with others. This is the overall reason for this book: to share what I have found within the pages of Scripture that would allow every Christian to face anything that this world can dish out with the fearlessness that all those Bible heroes demonstrated.

Before I really begin, I think that it is important that we define the term *fear* so that you the reader and I the writer are talking about the same thing. For that purpose, then, I like the definition from the *Holman Bible Dictionary*. That dictionary defines *fear* as "*a broad range of emotions that embrace both the secular and the religious worlds. Secular fear is the natural feeling of alarm caused by the expectation of imminent danger, pain, or disaster. Religious fear appears as the result of awe and reverence toward a supreme power.*"[1] As is too often the case, one English word is used to translate several different Hebrew and Greek words that all have their own nuance on the idea of fear or of being afraid.

By my count, there are ten Hebrew nouns and eight verbs that are regularly translated as "fear," "to fear," and "to be afraid." As we come to each of them, I will point out the different words and briefly explore their meaning as we look to fully understand what it means to live a fearless life in Christ. Only one of each, though, is most commonly found throughout the Old Testament, and both find their common root in yr (the noun being *yir'âh*[2] or mora and the verb *yârê*[3]). The noun and verb most commonly utilized in the Greek New Testament is *phŏbŏs*[4] and *phŏbĕŏ*[5] respectively. *Yir'âh* can range from general uneasiness to the extreme fear or terror that is

---

1. Trent C. Butler (general editor), *Holman Bible Dictionary* (Nashville, TN: Holman Bible Publishers, 1991), 480.
2. Strong's 3374.
3. Strong's 3373.
4. Strong's 5401.
5. Strong's 5399.

8

experienced when the loss of life seems imminent (see Jonah 1:10 when the sailors believed that their ship was going to sink due to the storm), while *phŏbŏs* also can follow that extreme range it also has the added dimension of dread (see Luke 21:26 on people's reaction when Christ returns). Eugene Merrill points out that there are no separate Hebrew or Greek terms that are solely used in describing the fear of God, so it can be assumed that this kind of fear is the same type of reaction that can be observed or felt from any happenstance with either a surprising, unusual, or threatening entity. It is believed that over time, fear of God or of manifestations of God and His power and authority became their own subcategory of fear, and this led to a special nuance of reverential awe or worshipful respect, which then became the preeminent concept.[6]

Secular fear is all around us and, when under control, is actually a very useful thing to keep us alive and unharmed. As a police officer, I have had the opportunity to speak to numerous citizen groups about various safety issues. One of the things that I regularly pointed out is that far too many people find themselves in untenable situations because they ignored some subtle signs or just a general uneasy feeling, what I liked to call the "hair on the back of the neck" warning. Of the thousands of crimes that I investigated over a twenty-seven-plus-year career, one of the most common recurring statements from a victim was that one of their five senses had tried to alert them to possible danger but that they had ignored it to their own peril. This is when some level of fear is actually quite useful. It is when we stay in that place of fear and see the proverbial bogeyman everywhere we are that we cease to function as we were designed to. We become frozen in place, trying to stop or mitigate situations that we either imagine are there or are real to some degree but out of our ultimate control.

The Bible deals a lot with secular fears and points out or assumes that most of them are natural. Some of these fears are the natural fear

---

6. Eugene H. Merrill, *Baker's Evangelical Dictionary of Biblical Theology*, ed. by Walter A. Elwell (copyright 1996 by Walter A. Elwell), published by Baker Books, a division of Baker Book House Company in Grand Rapids, Michigan, USA.

of humans by animals (Genesis 9:2) or the fear of some animals by humans (Amos 3:8) and the fear of other humans either on a personal level (Judges 9:21) or as one country may fear another more powerful or aggressive country (2 Chronicles 17:10). Particularly in relation to the latter and what is so evident in the world today are the natural fear of wars (Exodus 14:10), enemies especially those that are close at hand (Deuteronomy 2:4), and subjugation by another people (Deuteronomy 7:18). We will examine each of these and see how they fit into the Christian worldview. The Bible also addresses normal fears of the human condition such as death (Deuteronomy 28:66), disaster (Isaiah 43:2), the onset of sudden panic (Proverbs 3:25), fear of the unknown (Genesis 19:30), and being overwhelmed by adversity (Job 6:21). Again, the Bible sees these fears as normal to humans within their present fallen state. It does not, though, see these normal fears as the controlling condition to human life. These also, of course, will be brought into the light where fear has a difficult time existing.

Religious fear, or the awe and reverence that is due to God as Creator and Savior, is the other major theme and use of the English word *fear* and is especially prominent in the Old Testament and Hebrew thought, but it is also found within the New Testament. This can be seen when Paul instructs believers to work out their salvation with fear and trembling (Philippians 2:12). Thus, Paul and other New Testament writers are able to link the love of God toward us with the fear of God. This fear or awe is always the natural human response when a person finds himself in the presence of God when a person fully sees the reality of God's holiness in comparison to their own sin-caused inadequacy.

The fear of God or of His manifestations can be found in the Bible both in an abstract way, as in when just the idea of God alone is able to generate this kind of response or in historically recorded situations such as a theophany or a preformed miracle, that produces fear as an awe and reverence for God. The latter can be observed in the nation of Israel's opinion of God after their exodus deliverance experience (Exodus 14:31) and the reaction of Zechariah, the father of John the Baptist, after he saw the angel of the Lord (Luke 1:12).

The more common way that the reverential fear of God can be seen in the reactions of God's people is as they contemplate who He is and what He has done either in their own life or in the lives of people around them. This awe and reverence response to God and what He does is of such importance as a part of both biblical life and faith that it even can be observed as a description of God Himself. In Genesis 31:42, Jacob describes the Lord as the "Fear of Isaac," his father. This suggests that Isaac had such strong reverential submission to the Lord that, to him, God was the embodiment of fear. More commonly seen in Scripture, though, is that this type of fear or respect becomes the impetus for proper obedience and service in the life of a person. Thus, to fear God is to be obedient to His will. This idea of obedience from awe and respect can be especially found in Deuteronomy within the covenant descriptions. In each case, there is a directive to serve or obey God as a physical recognition of God's sovereignty. God, as Lord and King, properly demands and deserves the complete respect of His creation that can be best observed in obedient service.

The good news is that the reverential fear of God brings the reward of successful living in the here and now of life. Within the portion of the Bible known as wisdom literature (Job, Psalms, Proverbs, Ecclesiastes, and Song of Songs [or Solomon]) tells us that this kind of fear is the beginning wisdom and that it is seen as knowledge of the Holy One (Proverbs 9:10, 1:7 and Psalms 111:10). Thus, it becomes an interchangeable concept that to fear God is to know Him correctly and that to know Him completely and correctly is to fear Him. The result, then, is that a person who fears God is a person who is able to praise God (Psalms 22:23; Revelation 14:7), experience the blessing and benefits that come from God (Psalms 34:9, Psalms 103:11, Psalms 103:13, and Psalms 103:17), rest in the peace and security of God's protection (Psalms 112:7–8), and have one's days here on Earth prolonged (Proverbs 10:27 and 19:23). Of course, there is also the negative side, as this awe and respect for the power and authority of God can also produce a true fear of the inevitable wrath and punishment for those who do not know Him or choose to ignore Him or just simply refuse to obediently serve Him. So a proper reading and understanding of the Bible will show that there are two sides to the fear of the Lord coin. The first side is that which produces obedience from the awe and reverence of a holy God, and the opposite side is that which will cause a person to fall into despair and terror as they anticipate the justifiable action that his displeasure brings.

The purpose of this book, then, is to use Scripture to give the reader a monthly dose of why fear of any created thing or situation should not be the controlling aspect to a believer's life and to be a reference that can be used time and time again when fear seeks to be in control. The second and equally important purpose is to show what a healthy fear or correct concept of God should be and what that looks like. Christians should be and can be the most fear-free people on the planet. Psalm 27:1 HCS says, "The LORD is my light and my salvation—whom should I fear? The LORD is the stronghold of my life—of whom should I be afraid?"

Unless noted, all Bible quotes are from the Holman Christian Standard Bible (HCS).

January

> After these events, the word of the LORD
> came to Abram in a vision: Do not be afraid,
> Abram. I am your shield; your reward will be
> very great. (Genesis 15:1)

Oscar Wilde is the originator of the often-used line "No good deed goes unpunished." But just because he was the first to give that idea a memorable tagline does not mean that the concept has not been around for as long as there have been people. The very first "Fear not" in the Bible is addressed to Abraham in Genesis 15:1, which reads, *"After these events, the word of the LORD came to Abram in a vision: Do not be afraid, Abram. I am your shield; your reward will be very great."* It is the "after these events" that aligns Abraham with the "no good deed goes unpunished" quote.

At this point in the biblical narrative, Abraham had just returned from rescuing his nephew Lot after a battle in which Bera, the king of Sodom (where Lot was living) and four other kings were defeated by Chedorlamer and his three king allies. Abraham and his 318 trained men not only defeated the armies of these four city-states but also regained all the property and the people that had been taken during the campaign. What is remarkable is that he did not keep any of it for himself, even after it was offered to him, and only after offering 10 percent to Melchizedek who was "a priest to God most high" (Genesis 14:18) did he return everything to the rightful owners who had just been defeated in the original battle. But having accomplished this, it appears that perhaps Abraham began to have thoughts about the possible retaliation that he and his household might face.

After all, this was not his fight. He was not aligned with either side and was just rescuing his nephew who had elected to live in Sodom.

God, who sees the heart of man (1 Samuel 16:7), knew that Abraham was having some troubled thoughts about what might be coming and so He spoke to him in a vision and tells him to "fear not." God was addressing the "what if" kind of fear—the fear of the unknown, of what is coming next, and "will I be ready for it?" If you are the least bit normal and have lived for any amount of time on this planet, you have experienced this kind of fear. But let's call it what it really is: a fear of not being in control. Or it is the fear of being the recipient of bad events and circumstances that you don't deserve and are powerless to stop from occurring. This kind of fear finds its origins in a lack of knowledge. Abraham was most likely starting to wonder if and when Chedorlamer and his allies would retaliate and then when would it happen and finally how would it happen. It is really almost funny, isn't it? With only 318 men, he had just sent four kings and their armies hightailing it out of the area with nothing to show for their troubles but instead of enjoying his victory. Abraham was not enjoying the victory and high-fiving his men; he was starting to worry about what was coming next.

I have seen this kind of fear crop up really fast when someone gets involved with helping a stranger out during a violent crime. I have been told many times when I am interviewing witnesses that they do not want to be mentioned in the report or do not want to even look at a photo lineup to identify the criminal because they are afraid of the possible repercussions. They are afraid of the unknown, of what might happen if they are forced to testify in open court and do not want to be punished for having done a good deed. For the Christian, this is nothing more than a lack of faith in God to be in control of everything that goes on. How quickly we forget even after a great and improbable victory like the one that Abraham experienced. We quickly turn to trying to peer into the future, and when we can't, we start to become afraid like Abraham did. But notice how God answered that. He told Abraham that He would be Abraham's shield or his defense, so he did not have any business being afraid of what might or might not happen. The shields of Abraham's day were usually round and made of wicker or leather stretched over wooden frames with handles on the inside.[7] They were very maneuverable and offered some measure of protection, but not total. God, though, told Abraham that He would be his shield and such a complete shield that Abraham could be given the directive to not be afraid because, you see, Abraham was not going to be holding up this shield to protect himself. God was going to do it.

Later in the New Testament in Ephesians 6, the apostle Paul described the armor of God, and he notes that the shield that Christians use to defend themselves from attack is faith (Ephesians 6:16). This makes a lot of sense to me. When the enemy is shooting arrows at you from a distance or is trying to stab or cut you when he gets close, it takes a lot of faith to hold your ground and trust that your shield is not only going to be in the right place at the right time, but it is also going to be able to stop what is coming at you. So God essentially tells Abraham to have faith in him to give Abraham and his household the protection that they need. But that is a little difficult for most of us to do, isn't it? To really trust in protection that most of the time we cannot see or touch or manipulate ourselves. Even if we can, it takes a lot of discipline to hold your shield up and advance on the opponent who means to do us harm.

My son has recently become involved with the Society for Creative Anachronism, which is essentially a whole lot of guys that dress up in armor, live in tents for a few days, and have battles in which you can get "killed" but just like in a lot of video games: you are alive and good-to-go for the next day's melee. He told me that without a good shield, "you are essentially screwed" and won't last very long when the battle begins. The other thing that he told me is that unlike the TV and movie depictions, a lot of the ancient battles (and the battles that he is involved in) are just a big shoving match until something breaks down, and it isn't until you get the enemy to turn and run that the killing begins. You see, you are constantly try-

---

7. Trent C. Butler (general editor), *Holman Bible Dictionary* (Nashville, TN: Holman Bible Publishers, 1991), 103.

ing to get to your opponents unshielded back either through a deft move around his flank or by getting him to turn and run.

When you read the story in Genesis 14, you see this is exactly how Abraham and his men accomplished the victory. They attacked the larger force at night, and in the confusion, surprise got them to turn and run. Now the chase and the slaughter were on, which allowed Abraham to recover all the property and people. Shields are only good when you are facing the enemy, not when you are running away. But God told Abraham that He would be his shield, and that implied that it would always be in the right place at the right time and there would never be a need to turn and run. But notice that God didn't stop there; He told Abraham that as a result of his obeying the directive to not be afraid and to trust that God would be his shield, his reward for obedience would be very great. Remember that Abraham had just passed on a reward that would have rightly been his to take, but God told him to not be afraid and to trust in God's protection. As you examine the biblical narrative after this, you will find that Abraham does indeed become fabulously wealthy, but even more so, he is rewarded with a son and becomes the spiritual and physical father to millions of people through his sons Isaac and Ishmael because of his faith. God stays true to His word, as Abraham and his personal household never taste defeat or oppression from an outsider. It is this great faith that the writer of Hebrews says, "Now faith is the reality of what is hoped for, the proof of what is not seen" (Hebrews 11:1). God said, "Don't be afraid. I am your shield and nothing is going to get through me to harm you." Even though Abraham could not see it or hold it or even weld it in his own defense, his faith told him that it was there, and time proved that faith to be true. There is no reason for fear when God is shielding you.

*   *   *   *   *

And he said, "I heard You in the garden
and I was afraid because I was naked, so I hid."
(Genesis 3:10)

I have been fortunate to have been able to travel to Ndola, Zambia, to do a number of projects in support of Northrise University. At the conclusion of each trip, a group of us have then arranged to take a photo safari in a game preserve to see the animals that most people only get to see in a zoo. On my very first such expedition, our group was heading back to the small airstrip in a couple of open-air Land Rovers to begin our long trip back home when we came upon a pride of lions with a couple of young cubs. We had been warned that if we did encounter any predators, we were to remain rather still as the animals had become somewhat accustomed to seeing the vehicles and did not view them as either pray or enemies; but if you separated yourself from the vehicle, by standing up, for example, the safety of being in proximity to the vehicle would no longer hold true. One member of our group wanted to get a better picture and initially contemplated trying to move around to do so but was again warned by our driver that this would endanger all of us. I then remembered the joke that our host had told us by the campfire on our first night in the bush. He said that two visitors were on a recent jungle safari without a guide when suddenly a ferocious lion jumped in front of them. "Keep calm," the first explorer whispered. "Remember what we read in that book on wild animals of Africa? If you stand perfectly still and look the lion in the eye, he will turn and run."

"Sure," replied his buddy, "you've read the book, and I've read the book. But has the lion read the book?"

Fear, or being afraid, and disobedience often seem to go hand-in-hand. Adam did not know what fear was until he disobeyed God's directive. The very first time that we see Adam being afraid is right after he committed his first sin. He heard God's presence in the garden and tried to hide from Him. And like a parent playing hide-and-go-seek with their young child who is standing in almost plain sight, God calls out, "*Where are you?*" to which Adam replies, "*I heard You in the garden and I was afraid because I was naked, so I hid*" (Genesis 3:10). Prior to his disobedience, Adam and God had a very personal relationship. God had previously formed the animals and birds and then, as a part of his work in the garden, had Adam name them (Genesis 2:19–20). He gave Adam the directive about not eating from only two trees in all of Eden, ánd Adam complied. But God knew that Adam would not do well as the only creature of his kind, so He made Eve, and things still went along well until the temptation by the serpent (who is none other than Satan himself (Revelation 12:19) in which we saw the classic opening line in which the serpent changed God's directive to which Eve correctly responds with what God actually said. But then for some unknown reason, Eve added to God's command to not only eat from the two trees but also that they were not even allowed to touch them or they would die. So now with God's Word being changed, the serpent told the perfect lie, which is a lie core surrounded by a truth shell. Her pride was activated, and she now believed the serpent over God and took a bite. While this was problematic in and of itself, what really bothers me was that Adam was standing right there and let this all go on. Then when Eve didn't drop to the ground dead, he went ahead a took a bite as well (Genesis 2:6). Apparently, his pride was in full force as well, but he was willing to let Eve be the guinea pig before he jumped in as well. Some hero our first man was, huh? Eve was deceived, but Adam acted willfully.

And now the lie's effect was set. The truth shell (they would know good and evil) was there, but the lie core (this would allow them to be like God) was shown to be false. What they now knew instead was that their pride had separated them from their relationship with God. Shame set in as their actions left them exposed, and with that fear, came also. So Adam and Eve hid like young children standing in the middle of the room with their hands over their faces. But God sought them out anyway, not willing that mankind should stay lost. Even after the very first sin, we see God's grace as He makes the effort to seek the lost. Prior to this, the Bible points out that Adam and Eve were naked (exposed) but were not ashamed (Genesis 2:25). The Hebrew word that we translate as "ashamed" is *bûwsh* and means "to pale."[8] In my career, I have observed this quite often. As I make the arrest and tell the person what crime that I believe they have committed, they would often pale and become ashamed and feel the need to explain to me why they did what they did. This can

---

[8.] Strong's 954.

even apply to some really hardened criminals, especially when they're alone and do not feel like they have to keep up a facade of toughness for someone else.

Have you ever done that? Felt so much shame about something that you've done that you consciously avoid the very person who, while possibly being very disappointed, still loves you? When we are involved in sin, we try to hide something. Either we try to hide the sin itself, or if that is not possible, then we try to hide ourselves either literally or figuratively. Both these attempts, which are never completely successful, are really unhealthy to our hearts and minds. The good news, or the gospel if you will, is that as far as God is concerned, we don't have to seek Him out, as He is seeking us out and has already taken care of the punishment that disobedience brings. There is no reason to be afraid because the punishment is already over.

*   *   *   *   *

She was afraid. (Genesis 18:15)

The next person who is described in the Bible as being afraid is Sarah in Genesis 18:15, which reads, "*Sarah denied it. 'I did not laugh,' she said, because she was afraid. But He replied, 'No, you did laugh.'*" To put that verse into context, Sarah is old, past the age of childbearing (Genesis 18:11), and is listening to her husband Abraham having a conversation with three men, which turn out to be God and two angels. (This preincarnate visiting by God is called a theophany and happens a number of times in the Old Testament.) The Lord tells Abraham that He will come back in about a year, and at that time, Sarah will have a son. Sarah heard this and laughed to herself because she believed, and with good reason, that this wasn't possible because she was too old. This is a fairly common human reaction by the way. When we hear something that is blatantly ridiculous, many of us chuckle, either openly or inside our heads, at the dumb thing we just heard. The problem, though, is that God knew and called her out on it. Abraham was treating these men with honor, serving them one of his calves, and having fresh bread made for them. The last thing that would have been culturally appropriate then would be for Sarah to openly dispute or mock what they said. She thought she could get away with it due to her distance, but God knew what she was thinking and why. His challenge wasn't so much that she laughed but what it showed: her lack of faith in God to work outside of normalcy.

Sarah was engaged in what is known as uniformitarianism, which basically means that how things are and will be are based solely on what has happened in the past. She was old, too old to have children, and now some stranger was telling her that in about a year, she would not only have a child, but it would also be a son. She did not believe either that God would or could allow her to be a mother. Like most people, she had either forgotten or never been told that God had created everything, but since she had not observed God doing anything like that now, she went with the uniform way of thinking. Everything is set, and nothing can or will change. What a powerless god that would be.

To move past a lot of our fear, we need to remember that God has not gone out of the creation business. Sometimes we miss seeing this even when it is happening right in front of us. A great illustration of this is the well-known Bible story about the feeding of the five thousand that we find in all four gospel accounts.[9] And of course, the five thousand just refers to the men in attendance with women and children present. That number could well have doubled or tripled, so we are probably talking in the ten to fifteen thousand people range or roughly the size of a full Wells Fargo Arena (capacity of fourteen thousand) where my hometown Arizona University Sun Devil basketball team plays.

As the story goes, Jesus has been speaking to the crowd for some time, and it is getting late in the day, and His disciples come to him and tell Him that He needs to wrap it up so that the crowd can go and get something to eat. Jesus replies that His disciples should give the crowd something to eat, and when they reply that they cannot, He asks what resources that they do have. In John's gospel, chapter 6,

---

[9.] Matthew 14:13–21, Mark 6:31–44, Luke 9:11–17, and John 6:1–13.

we learn that one young lad had come prepared and had five barley loaves and two small fish that he was apparently willing to share. Now don't let your idea of a loaf be the foot-long item that you buy in the local grocery store. We are talking more like an individual roll here. Jesus directs the crowd to sit in groups of fifty, and then He prays over the meal and begins breaking up the bread and the fish and starts feeding the crowd. He continues to do this until not only is everyone fed, but also twelve baskets of leftovers are gathered up! Did you see what Jesus was doing? He was creating food on the spot and not just the raw materials but ready-for-consumption barley bread and fish.

God still creates today, and we miss it in our uniformitarianism view of the world. Because we understand the process of sex and reproduction, we assume that God no longer has a direct role in the creation of life. Psalm 102:18 tells us—and this will be a surprise to some of you—that God has been creating humans ever since the first seven days of creation, and there are many more of us who shall be created for God's ultimate glory! James J. S. Johnson, JD, ThD, in his article "'New from Nothing': Is God Still Creating Today?" writes this:

> Although our procreated physical bodies are meticulously and carefully "woven" from preexisting genetic information, biochemically written on and "housed" within biochemical materials, the non-material part of each one of us—soul, spirit, personality (or whatever terms are proper for describing the non-physical part of every person)—was specially "created" by God.[10]

---

[10]. J. J. S. Johnson, "'New from Nothing': Is God Still Creating Today?" (2013) *Acts & Facts*, 42 (5): 10–11. Online at http://www.icr.org/article/7396.

If Sarah knew her God like that, she would not have laughed or had a reason to be afraid. There is no reason to be afraid because God is still creating.

*   *   *   *   *

He feared to dwell in Zoar. (Genesis 19:30)

There is a difference in being afraid to be somewhere and being cautious and aware of your surroundings. One of the life attitudes that permeates the life of most experienced police officers is to not have your back exposed to a threat of any kind at any time. Thus, you will commonly find when an officer sits in a restaurant that he or she will try to have their back to a wall and, if possible, a clear line of sight to the main entrance. My own wife and family have acquiesced to this way of doing things in my life and will, if it is possible, keep that seat available for me when we are dining out. It just makes me more comfortable. There have been times, though, where I was just flat scared to be somewhere. Remember that issue I have with spiders? On one particular call, I had to go under a mobile home to look for some evidence that had possibly been hidden in the crawl space between the bottom of the mobile home and the ground. It was a maze of spider webs, and in Arizona, we have one particular little nasty spider called a black widow that is very venomous and has a very sticky and disorganized web. I made very short work of that search and concluded that if none of the webs were disturbed, nothing bigger than the spiders in residence had been under there in quite some time. Even though I was under the mobile home for just a few moments, I felt the webs on me for the rest of the night and was constantly checking myself to make sure that I had not picked up any unwanted eight-legged hitchhikers.

Lot, Abraham's nephew, was afraid to live in a town called Zoar after the destruction of Sodom where he had been living. To put Lot's story in context, God sent two angels to get him and his family out of Sodom, as He was planning on destroying the five cities of the plains of which Sodom and Gomorrah were the most prominent. Lot was directed to flee to the mountains, but he requested to go to the smallest of the five cities, Zoar. The angel granted the request, and Lot and his two daughters ended up there. Lot's wife had already failed to turn her back on her old life and had been turned into a pillar of salt as God destroyed the cities and their inhabitants for the unbridled evil that they were known for. When that destruction was complete, the very next thing that we read in Genesis 19 is that Lot decided to go to the mountains after all, as he was now afraid to live in Zoar. What made him afraid? We really don't know. Speculation by Bible commentators is that either Lot observed the same wickedness in Zoar that he had seen in Sodom and the other cities and thought that the same destruction would happen there. The other idea is that the people of Zoar would blame him and his household for the destruction of their sister cities that no doubt had friends and relatives in them. If the men of Zoar were anything like those in Sodom, Lot had a very reasonable fear. But whatever is the case, Lot, due to fear either real or imagined, made a short stay in Zoar and headed for the mountains where he was told to go in the first place.

Lot is a hard guy to get a good grasp on. We know from 2 Peter 2:7–8 that he was a righteous man who was living in the midst of a wicked place and bothered by it, and yet he chose not to extricate himself from the situation. As a result, he lost everything. He had no credibility with his sons-in-law; he lost his wife and his life's work along with his fortune and very nearly his own life. Even his character took a strong hit as we left him in the Bible narrative, allowing his daughters to get him drunk so that they could be impregnated by him. He was also obviously having some faith issues of his own. Even though God had sent the two angels to rescue him from the destruction that had just come to Sodom and Gomorrah, he found himself afraid to live in the place he had asked to go to. How quickly we can forget God's power to preserve us, and the result is fear.

How often does our fear come about like that? We are in a place that we know we shouldn't be, but we make excuses for it and continue on anyway. Then when something happens, we are totally freaked out as we find ourselves beyond our resources to deal with the situation and we lose sight of God's ability to preserve us, and fear becomes the controlling emotion of the moment. And rarely is fear the impetus for good decision-making. Instead, the natural response of fight-or-flight sets in, and if rational thought doesn't take hold quickly, we can find ourselves in an even worse predicament, like Lot did in a cave with his two daughters whom had obviously been more influenced by the ways of their neighbors than the righteous attitude of their father.

For a while, I was a regular speaker for my police department, and one of the most requested topics was how to protect oneself or to prevent, as much as possible, being a crime victim. I developed a teaching outline on this subject that I called the PORE method. It stands for preparation, observation, reaction, and evaluation. Under the preparation portion, I talked about not only the physical preparation (exercise, proper diet, drinking plenty of water every day) but also the mental and spiritual preparation to see yourself surviving whatever situation confronts you. Lot failed in this area, as he apparently maintained his own righteousness but no longer had communion with anyone else who did.

Next was observation. Here I told my audience to be constantly aware of their surroundings and to trust the little hairs on the back of their necks. Of all the hundreds of victims that I have interviewed over the years, a great deal of them have told me that just prior to the event that one of their five senses had alerted them to something. In almost every case, though, the next thing that they told me was that they had ignored it and gone on with what they were doing until suddenly the bad guy did his thing. Lot failed in this area, as he observed the evil going on around him and was disturbed by it but apparently made excuses for it and stayed in the midst of it.

The third area is reaction, and it was here that I told my audiences about crime scene 1 and crime scene 2. Crime scene 1 is a bad place, and the crime is in motion. At this place, I told my audiences that you *may* get assaulted, you *may* get killed, and if you are a woman you *may* get raped. Crime scene 2, though, is worse. This is the place the criminal wants to get you to, and then all the mays that you just read change to "will." For whatever reason, the criminal is more comfortable doing those activities in crime scene 2, which is why they want you there so your reaction needs to be in crime scene 1. Whether that is fight, flight, screaming, deadly force, or something else, it is best done while the word *may* is still in effect. Lot failed in this area as well, as we know from 2 Peter 2 that his observation ability was in effect but that he failed to properly react. He failed to remove himself from a situation that verses 7 and 8 say he was distressed by the unrestrained behavior of the immoral (for as he lived among them, that righteous man tormented himself day by day with the lawless deeds he saw and heard).

The fourth area is evaluation. As I pointed out to my audiences, this can only be completed by a survivor. Dead people cannot evaluate anything. But all too often what I had observed was people getting stuck in the blame game and often with themselves as the main culprit as they assessed what they had done wrong. What I told them was to try to first and foremost concentrate and maybe even physically write down what they had done right. Even if it was just one or two things, as there would be plenty of time later for self-recriminations. This was so that they could build upon and reinforce those things that they had done right so as to bolster their reactions in the future. Lot failed in this area as well. Instead of evaluating the situation and observing how God had preserved him in the midst of a huge disaster and moving closer to God, he instead gave way to fear and, as a result, soon found himself the father of his own two grandsons who became the Moabites and the Ammonites who were ungodly people that history tells us would constantly harass their cousins, the people of Israel.

There is no reason for fear when we are consistently preparing our hearts for worship and obedience, observing what is less than God's standards in our lives, reacting by avoiding or removing ourselves from ungodly situations, and correctly evaluating what God has done and is doing in our lives and having the faith the He will continue to do so.

FEBRUARY

> Now I know that you fear God. (Genesis
> 22:12)

The above quote is from Genesis 22:12 and is God speaking to Abraham just after stopping him from sacrificing Isaac. While this story has always been especially poignant to me, it really didn't completely take hold until I became a father. Unlike Abraham, I have been blessed with five children—four girls and one boy—and I'll tell you right now that even at their worst, I could not kill any of them; and again, unlike Abraham, I'm glad God has never asked me to prove my reverence, my fear for Him in that way. Even in those times when they intentionally failed to live up to the standards that we had established for our family and brought shame and embarrassment to themselves and us, they were still my children. Plus, it was during those rough times that I really clung to Proverbs 22:6 (*"Teach a youth about the way he should go; even when he is old he will not depart from it"*) and God's mercy to me as a woefully inadequate parent and the Creator and Sustainer of the lives that He had brought into the world.

The fear here in this verse is the main Hebrew verb *yârê* and has the idea of reverential awe to something that is beyond you, more powerful than you, and virtually unexplainable. God has tested Abraham with his only son Isaac and found that Abraham has the right concept of the God he serves. In the *Bible Knowledge Commentary* (by the Dallas Seminary Faculty), this fear of God means "to reverence Him as sovereign, trust Him implicitly, and obey Him without question."[11] This is what Abraham did in building the altar, getting the wood ready, and then binding and laying Isaac on the altar and getting the knife. He obeyed without question. No fear.

We already discussed in the last chapter that Abraham and Sarah were old, too old to naturally be parents. But God had made them a promise and not only that they would have a son but that Abraham's descendants would be as innumerable as the stars and the sand. So Abraham had to really believe that if he carried out God's directive to sacrifice Isaac, God would somehow restore him to life. That's the fear of God in its purest form: complete trust in what God said (lots of descendants) and complete trust in what He asked him to do (sacrifice) and that He would not allow one to affect the other. Abraham immortalized the place with a new name for God, calling him Yahweh Yir'eh, meaning "The Lord will provide." This getting the right level of reverential awe or fear of God is something that we all struggle with. There was a big movement a number of years ago within the Christian church to view God as a friend or buddy. While God is our friend, He is so much more than that, and we would do well to constantly remind ourselves that we serve and worship the God who created everything with His word and held it together until the last day. That He chose to be our friend is just a bonus really.

The word *reverence*, or its more common cousin *respect*, is a much overused or, perhaps better, an improperly used word in our society. I hear it constantly among the criminal element that I deal with on a daily basis where instead of its proper definition of "to consider worthy of high regard,"[12] it has devolved to something akin to "because I exist, you should be nice to me and not hurt my feelings." Thus, if I accuse them of the crime that I am charging them with, I am disrespecting them in some form or fashion. There has been many a homicide or an aggravated assault because of one person's view on whether or not someone else has properly, in their opinion, shown them respect. We are all still alive only because God's mercy

---

[11] *Bible Knowledge Commentary: Old Testament* (Colorado Springs, CO: Cook Communications Ministries, 2004), ed. by John F. Walvoord, Roy B. Zuck, 65.
[12] https://www.merriam-webster.com/dictionary/respect.

has allowed us to avoid the penalty for our lack of proper respect or reverential awe to the God of creation.

Abraham got it right. Everything and everyone else in our lives is to take a backseat to how we view God. Once we get that right, then obedience to His commands becomes a done deal. Abraham demonstrated that he was not afraid to completely trust God and be obedient even in the face of the appearance that his actions would negate God's promise to him. We do not need to have any fear when we are properly viewing God with the reverence that He is due and being obedient as a result.

*   *   *   *   *

Told all these things in their ears: and the
men were sore afraid. (Genesis 20:8)

Hearing something from someone and becoming afraid is best illustrated by the old story of Chicken Little. After an acorn hits him in the head, he runs around and tells all the other animals that the sky is beginning to fall until he gets the entire barnyard in a panic. In that story, one small animal affects one farm, and the panic is limited to that location. Thanks to the internet and instant worldwide communication, a modern-day Chicken Little now has a much wider effect, as the warning gets shared and forwarded almost instantly. I, like almost everyone else, regularly get e-mail and Facebook messages from otherwise right-minded friends and acquaintances who are seeking to pass on a warning that they received from someone else, often with the accompanying tag line that they're not sure if it's true or not, but they are sending it on "just to be safe." For a while, I would regularly visit rumor-busting sites like *Snopes.com* and *ThatsNonsense.com* and then try to stop the rumor, but I soon discovered that the truth would often die in the face of fear-based forwarding and sharing. One of my favorite such passed-along fears of 2016 was the Facebook privacy notice. The claim was that all of a person's posts on Facebook will become public and that the only way to prevent it from happening (or to prevent Facebook from using your information) was to copy and paste the attached legal privacy notice to your own timeline. I cannot begin to recall how many of those "just in case" posts that I saw my friends and family place. Chicken Little strikes again, and this time, it's global.

In the case of Abimelech, though, in the above-quoted verse, what the men heard that made them so afraid wasn't rumor, it came straight from the source; so they had every right to be afraid. Abraham's story picks up right after the destruction of the cities of the plain and Lot's ignoble end. He and Sarah had moved south, and the local king, Abimelech, took Sarah into his harem because Abraham was afraid and kind of lied about Sarah being his sister instead of his wife. Like all really good lies, there was truth here, as she was his half sister. So he did not directly lie, but he intentionally withheld the pertinent facts out of fear. But if you know his story, this isn't the first time that he used this story. Early on in his journey, he wound up in Egypt and did the same thing, and essentially, the same results happened. You can lie while telling the truth if your intent is to deceive and you cherry-pick the truths that you tell. I know this personally as I, like my father before me, am a master at this type of truth-lying. I'm not bragging but admitting one of my deeper faults.

So God intervenes and keeps Sarah's purity intact so that there is no question as to her offspring and God's plan. God comes to Abimelech in a dream and tells him that he's a dead man for the capital offense of adultery with another man's wife. Abimelech pleads his case, and God tells him that He knows how it all happened and that Abimelech should restore Sarah to the prophet Abraham (first time in the Bible that this designation is used) and have him pray for Him so that he would live. God then gave the warning, though, that if Abimelech didn't restore Sarah to Abraham, He and "all who are yours"—i.e., his entire household—would die. This is the message that caused the men of his household to be sore afraid. Abimelech and his household apparently believed what God had said and not only obeyed and restored Sarah to Abraham, he also added sheep, oxen, servants, and a thousand pieces of silver and the right to live anywhere in his kingdom just to sweeten the deal. Abraham prayed, and the Bible recorded that Abimelech, his wife, and his female servants were all healed and began bearing children as God had withheld their ability to reproduce until Sarah was restored and Abraham prayed.

This all seems to make sense now. God tells you to do something and live or not do it and die, so you do it. And yet not everyone who hears God's directives believes that it's from God or that they need to do it to live. God's Word and His people have been telling a lost world for centuries what they needed to do to live and not die, and yet, unlike Abimelech and the men of his household, most have chosen to not choose God's one and only path to life and instead have chosen to disbelieve that they will die and be forever apart from their Creator and Sustainer and will choose their own path to heaven.

When we are told something by someone, we have to decide whether or not to believe what we have just heard. Not believing everything we hear and the polar opposite of believing everything are both dangerous and stupid places to be. The latter makes us susceptible to the Chicken Littles of the world, and the former will find us enmeshed in a disaster that we otherwise could have avoided by listening to a warning. But when God tells us something, we should not have to decide on whether or not to believe it. His track records on having something happen when and how He says it is going to be is an incredible 100 percent. Thus, when we read the promises in Scripture of God's unfailing and untiring protection for us, we should not be afraid when we hear anything that is contrary to God's word in the Bible.

*   *   *   *   *

He feared to say, she is my wife. (Genesis 26:7)

Like father, like son. Physical traits like size, hair color, face shape, and so forth are often shared between a father and his children. Many of you probably know of a family where all the children look more like copies of a parent than siblings. I attended a church some years ago that had an associate pastor with several children.

For him, there was no denying parentage, and for his children, there was no denying who their siblings were! But sometimes, it's not just physical traits but habits and ways of dealing with problems that get passed down from one generation to the next. In the case of Isaac, having a beautiful wife like his father did mean that when you get in a possibly hostile environment, you claim that she is your sister instead of your wife to protect your own skin.

At this point in the biblical narrative, there was a famine, and God told Isaac to not go to Egypt. Instead, he was to remain in the area, and God would bless him. So he ended up in the area of Gerar, just like when Abraham had gone south, in the area controlled by the Philistines. The local ruler was Abimelech (not the same from his father's incident; Bible scholars believe that the name is a dynastic title as opposed to a personal name), and the locals started asking about Rebekah, and Isaac became afraid for his own well-being. He had probably heard the stories growing up and now resorted to the same lie. But unlike Abraham, this was no truth-based lie. Rebekah was a cousin, not a half sister, and was already the mother of Esau and Jacob.

Unlike his predecessor, this Abimelech didn't need a personal message from God. Instead, God allowed him to providentially see Isaac and Rebekah alone together, and apparently, they were treating each other in a way that was indicative of a married couple instead of a brother and sister. The Bible doesn't specify what that was, so I'll leave it to your imagination to fill in the details of what Abimelech might have observed. Apparently, he figured it out quite quickly and confronted Isaac with the truth, and so we get the quote from Isaac about fearing to say that Rebekah was his wife. This Abimelech, who might have also heard the same stories from the prior Abimelech's viewpoint, quickly realized the danger and made sure that no one touched Rebekah. If I may, I'd like to pause for a moment and address the men who may be reading this. It is *never* in your best interest to disavow your wife. No matter what may be occurring or has occurred, she is your wife for better or for worse, and God's Word shows that He takes a dim view of men who fail to love their wife like He loves His body of believers known as the church.

Isaac then starts to really prosper, and the locals begin to be jealous of his success. There are repeated arguments over water rights to the wells that his servants have dug until he finally gets one far enough away from the local Philistines that they agree it can be his. All this constant turmoil has to be bothering Isaac because it is then that God appeared to him at night and told him to not be afraid as He was going to fulfill the promises to Abraham through him and that he, too, would be blessed and have his progeny multiplied. One has to wonder where Isaac got his fear from. He most likely knew the stories of Abraham's life and saw how God's hand was there. He had even recently had his lie exposed, but God had protected him even when he wasn't being honest and true. At no point in the biblical record do we see anything in Isaac's life that would have warranted this position of fear, and yet there it was. Like I described in the introduction, this appears to have all the earmarks of those shadow fears that exist just on the periphery of our awareness, the fears that are not based so much on facts as they are on possibilities. This may happen. That could happen. I'm aware that this happened to someone else, so might it not happen to me?

In the midst of all the worry and speculation, God comes to Isaac and bluntly says, "Do not be afraid, for I am with you." He's given a command and a reason it's a good idea to obey it. Decide to obey and to willingly not be afraid and the reason is none other than God Himself will be with him. God very consistently tells us the same thing: Stop looking at the shadows. Stop imagining the things that may or may not be there. "*I am with you.*" The apostle Paul, who seems to attract trouble like a magnet attracts steel, echoes this idea in Romans 8:31 when he wrote this: "*If God is for us, who is against us?*" God knows, and Paul understands that we humans can only see one thing at a time. We can only think about one thing at a time. And so we are told, in no uncertain terms, to not look at our fears, to not concentrate on them but to focus on the fact that God is with us. Our problem, though, is that we have very short memories and have to be reminded of this over and over again.

*   *   *   *   *

> He was afraid and said, "What an awesome place this is! This is none other than the house of God. This is the gate of heaven. (Genesis 28:17)

A few years ago, I got to go to Europe with my youngest daughter and a number of her classmates as a part of an AP Euro history course. Of the many impressive things that we saw, none were more impressive than the old cathedrals and churches, impressive stone buildings that have stood for hundreds of years and are chock-full of history. In one, they were playing a recording of the choir that normally performs. The sound was, in a word, incredible. As I looked across the great length of this mighty structure, I could imagine a full congregation and the sound of the choir bringing everyone within to a point that they could almost physically feel the presence of the divine. But then I have also been to Zambia, in the very heart of Africa, and stepped into a small church made out of sun-dried mud blocks in a small village. It was a building that would house no more than a couple of dozen worshipers at most and that, due to the effects of sun and rain, would have to be rebuilt every couple of decades. And yet in this simple and humble structure, especially when the local congregation began to sing, it felt like the most impressive cathedral that I had seen. No flying buttresses or gilded decorations. No impressive marble statuary remembering those long-dead members. I got the feeling that God was present there and that this was His house. And like Jacob before me, I thought, *What an awesome place this is!*

This verse that heads up this section is from the story of Jacob's life when he sleeps out in a field and uses a rock for a pillow while on his way to Haran to find a wife from his relatives as his father had instructed him to do. During the night, he has the vision of the stairway to heaven with angels going up and down. God spoke to him and restated the promise that He had made to both Abraham and Isaac about having numerous descendants. Then in Genesis 28:15, God makes this statement: *"Look, I am with you and will watch over you wherever you go. I will bring you back to this land, for I will not leave you until I have done what I have promised you."* This is a very personal and intimate promise. God is promising to be personally with Jacob on a permanent basis until His promises have been fulfilled. If that doesn't remove fear of the unknown future, then nothing will.

Jacob's reaction to this conversation is priceless. Upon waking, he realizes that God was there in the wilderness, and he did not know it. Then he was afraid perhaps because, like so many of us, he had relegated God to a particular location. But then notice his next statement from verse 17: "*What an awesome place this is! This is none other than the house of God.*" He wasn't standing in one of the great cathedrals of Europe. The temple in Jerusalem was still hundreds of years in the future. He is standing in the wilderness and suddenly, perhaps for the first time, sees it as an awesome place. Why? Because of the presence of God was in that place. I like the fact that Jacob's first reaction was fear, but in remembering the promise that God had made to him, his next immediate reaction was to see how awesome anywhere was when he realized that God was personally there. I have been in some pretty dark and dangerous places at times in my life, and tendrils of fear began to wind their way through my thoughts, constricting my ability to see what was actually in the place, God himself. When I really fully realized that there was no place that I could go that God was not there, my fear dissipated, and everywhere I went became an awesome place.

*   *   *   *   *

Please rescue me from the hand of my brother Esau, for I am afraid of him. (Genesis 32:11)

I have two brothers, and although we live in different places, on the infrequent times that we are able to get together, we remain friends; and within moments, we return to a younger version of ourselves, joking and making fun of one another. When we were boys, though, we averaged about one fight a day over nothing really. I think it began when we got up and ended at night when we went to bed. A house full of young testosterone means that everything devolves into a competition of some sort. Being the oldest, I had the inside edge, but I wasn't the fastest nor the strongest; my brothers held those places. And yet there was always a loyalty among us. No matter how much we were personally battling, if an outsider came at one of us, he got to face all three. I could knock one of my brothers senseless, but no one else had better lay a hand on them. This may resonate with a lot of you, as I have heard similar stories from other people from all over the world.

Sometimes, though, sibling rivalry can take a very nasty and sometimes deadly turn. In 2016, a seventy-year-old Baptist pastor, the Rev. William Schooler, was gunned down in his church by his sixty-eight-year-old brother Daniel in Dayton, Ohio. In 2001, fifteen-year-old Scott Turnlund killed his seventeen-year-old brother Nathan in their home and buried him in the backyard in Chelsea, Alabama. And as you look through history, if money or a throne is involved, being the wrong person's brother can be fatal. But thankfully, this tends to be the exception and not the norm. Now if I was to list the brothers who had merely assaulted brothers, sometimes severely, the list would fill several volumes.

For those who are not acquainted with the Bible story, Jacob had an older twin brother by the name of Esau. These two could not have been more different either physically or by temperament. Esau was outdoorsy and physically hairy. He was a hunter and a man who lived in the face of the danger by being in the wilderness. Scripture described Jacob, though, as smooth and a quiet man who stayed at home (Genesis 25:27). Jacob's mother, Rebekah, was partial to Jacob, while Isaac favored his manlier son Esau. Not a good recipe for a cohesive family unit. Another big difference in the brothers was that Esau tended to be a "right now" kind of guy, while Jacob was a bit shrewder with an eye to the future. That became evident one day when Esau came in from a long day in the field and was hungry. Jacob had prepared a lentil stew and Esau asked for some. Jacob told him that he will give him some if Esau would sell him his birthright right then and there. Before we go any further, you have to understand what this meant to the culture of that time and place. The birthright denoted authority and preeminence and a double portion of the inheritance when Isaac died.[13] But Esau, being the "right-now" kind of guy, decided that his being hungry took precedent over any future position. Of course, Isaac wasn't aware of this and likely, given his favoring of Esau, would have forbid it had he known. This would have been bad enough, but to ensure that Jacob would come out on top, he and his mother engaged in a bit of skullduggery as Isaac was dying and about to pronounce his blessing upon his sons.

Before I continue with their story, we have to back up a bit in the narrative and see that in Genesis 25 when Rebekah was pregnant with her twin boys, they were constantly battling for room in her womb. Apparently, she was pretty miserable and asked God why her pregnancy was going along like this. God responded in verse 23, *"Two nations are in your womb; two people will come from you and be separated. One people will be stronger than the other, and the older will serve the younger."* So she already knew that Esau would wind up serving Jacob, but like so many of us, she decided that God needed some help getting that prophecy to come about. This is kind of one of those "God helps those who help themselves" ways of thinking, a concept that is most decidedly not found in the Bible. So now back to the blessing from Isaac.

Isaac was old, blind, and dying, and he asked his boy Esau to go on a hunting trip and to prepare him some of the game to eat, and then he would bestow his official blessing. Rebekah overheard this conversation and decided to take matters into her own hands. She got Jacob and hatched a plan to fool Isaac. Jacob pointed out that there were some obvious differences between himself and his brother, but Rebekah had it all figured out. She had Jacob kill a lamb, and she prepared the savory food that he wanted. She knew that her husband was blind, but his nose still worked, so she had Jacob put on some of Esau's clothes. Then she put the skins of young goats on his hands and on the back of his neck because she knew that Isaac's sense of touch was still intact. Then Jacob went in to his father, smelling like his brother and hairy like his brother and with the food that

---

[13.] W. E. Vine, *Vine's Expository Dictionary of Old & New Testament Words* (Nashville, TN: Thomas Nelson Publishers, 2001), 120.

his father wanted, and promptly lied and said that he was Esau. Of course, they forgot the last of Isaac's five senses: his hearing. That and enough time hadn't elapsed for a hunt and the food preparation. Jacob told another quick lie to deal with the time issue. (Isn't that usually the case, a lie has to be backed up by another?) Isaac realized this, and he heard Jacob's voice; but now his nose and his ears were in disagreement, so he asked to touch his son. Jacob felt like Esau, so the tie is broken, but there's still some unsettled thought in Isaac's mind, so he asked Jacob again if he's really Esau. Jacob kept the lie going and gave his father the food. After the meal, he asked his son to come near and kiss him, and when he did so, Isaac smelled his clothes and settled it in his mind that this was Esau and pronounced his blessing.

Like the birthright, this is a big deal in the culture of the story. Once something was said, it took on a life of its own and could not be unsaid. The *Holman Bible Dictionary* notes that "blessing and cursing released suprahuman powers which could bring to pass the content of the curse or the blessing."[14] So when Isaac is blessing his son, it's a done deal when he finishes. And what a blessing it was. He pronounces material well-being, peoples serving him, being the master over his brethren, and that his mother's sons would bow down to him and that "those who curse you will be cursed, and those who bless you will be blessed" (Genesis 27:29). Jacob immediately takes off, having now secured the blessing to go along with the birthright, and just like in a well-timed comedy movie, Esau comes in with the prepared game that he had hunted. The same exchange of identification occurs, and now Isaac realizes what has happened and tells Esau that the blessing has already been pronounced. Esau realizes that Jacob has got him again and begs Isaac for a blessing. Isaac does so and lets him know that he will have to live by the use of his weapons and that he would serve Jacob but that eventually he would "break his yoke from your neck."

[14.] Trent C. Butler (general editor), *Holman Bible Dictionary* (Nashville, TN: Holman Bible Publishers, 1991), 198.

Esau is understandably mad and decides to kill his brother after the official time of mourning is over after the death of his father. Rebekah, though, gets wind of this and concocts a plan to get Jacob out of the area and sends him to his uncle. She then manipulates Isaac to agree that he left, and so Jacob is protected from Esau's murderous rage. Now fast forward at least twenty years. Jacob has married two of his cousins. (They were sisters, but his uncle pulled a fast one and switched them. So apparently, Rebekah and her brother Laban had a family trait of deceitfulness. This is starting to sound like a badly written soap opera, isn't it?) And due to some family issues, he takes his family and heads for home. The problem is, though, he has to pass by where Esau and his family now reside. Jacob sends a messenger ahead to tell Esau, but when the messenger gets back, he tells Jacob that Esau is personally coming out to meet him and bringing four hundred men with him. Jacob is understandably afraid, and so we read the verse at the start of this section. Apparently, it's payback time. But I'll take you to the finish. Esau greets his brother and lets him know that he no longer wants to kill his brother.

Jacob had every right to be afraid. He was dishonorable toward his brother on two separate occasions and had literally stolen the blessing that should have been Esau's. This is fear that again finds its birth in the evil that we have done. We stand condemned in our minds, and maybe justly so, because of how we've mistreated others. We know how we would like to respond if the situation is reversed. But what Jacob really did was fail to trust in the promise that he had received from God. for he also had been told that his descendants would be like *the sand of the sea* (Isaiah 32:12).

I see that a lot of my fear about people and situations stems from forgetting the promises of God. Essentially my fear says that He's too uncaring or impotent to see them through. I do like Jacob's response though. He sent lots of gifts of animals (meaning wealth) ahead of him to Esau although we don't know if he was just trying to manipulate his brother once again or if he was truly making a very visible apology by sharing his blessing with Esau. While I choose the latter position, I really can't defend it categorically. When we've wronged someone, and we know it, we should be the first to try to make it right. While that still may be a little scary, the alternative of having someone, especially a family member, justifiably angry with us should be far scarier.

*   *   *   *   *

> If the God of my father, the God of Abraham, the Fear of Isaac, had not been with me." (Genesis 31:42)

This is one of those different words for fear when we read "Fear of Isaac." The word is *pachad*,[15] and it implies the feeling of dread or the standing in awe of something. So we have an interesting phrase here. Jacob says "the God of his father" (Isaac), "the God of Abraham," and "the Fear of Isaac." So how is that different than what he already said? This is something personal. Jacob moves from the general concept of God to the personal relationship that he had observed in his father's life. His father had obviously viewed God with levels of dread (this comes from comparison) and awe in how awesome and powerful God was. Remember, it was his father who had accompanied his grandfather and had been placed on the altar to be sacrificed until God intervened at the last moment. Isaac had a view, an understanding if you will, of God that was very powerful, and it left him with a *pachad* concept of the God he served.

Seeing this kind of fear or reverential awe doesn't just happen in the life of a child. It has to be both taught and openly and genuinely lived out in their presence. Twice in the book of Deuteronomy we read this instruction: "*Teach them to your children, talking about them when you sit in your house and when you walk along the road, when you lie down and when you get up*" (Deuteronomy 6:7, 11:19). In fact, it uses the word *impress*. This is the same word that is used to describe the striking of one object into another that leaves an intentional mark, like the stamping of a coin. And notice that it is an all-day sort of thing. It can't be relegated to just Sunday mornings at the hands of

---

[15.] Strong's 6343.

a teacher for an hour. It is to come from us as parents all day all the time. They are to hear and see our fear of the Lord, so much so that it forms an impression on their hearts and minds. When our children experience this, it actually forms a level of confidence for them as it did for Jacob. They learn that they can depend on the God of their father as they hold Him in awe.

March

God said, "I am God, the God of your father. Do not be afraid to go down to Egypt, for I will make you into a great nation there." (Genesis 46:3)

Letting go of what we know and where we know can be a scary proposition. I am always amazed at those intrepid souls that can just pick up and move to an entire new community or country seemingly as easily as some people change a radio station in their car. I have lived in only two states, Southern California, where I lived for most of my grade school years, and Phoenix, Arizona, where I was born and have lived ever since middle school. As I already mentioned, I've been privileged to be able to travel outside of the US, but I have also been fortunate enough to have traveled to most of the fifty states and have seen some absolutely beautiful areas that for a fleeting moment I thought I'd like to move to. But I always return home without acting on those temporary thoughts. My children, though, do not seem to have been affected by this inability to just pick up and go. As I write this, I have children and the much more desirable grandchildren they have given me living in Colorado, North Dakota, Flagstaff (at least this is only two hours away!), and one at a Southern California university; and she has already announced that she does not see herself returning to Arizona as a permanent resident when she graduates. My son and his wife do live here, at least for now, so I've managed to hold on to one out of five.

The fear of leaving the known for the unknown can show up in other areas as well. Every time that I changed assignments within the Phoenix Police Department, I had that fear come up that I would not be adequate to the task. The idea that would float through my head was that the new environment that I found myself in would somehow be my undoing. Even after I was promoted to sergeant, every time I had to move to a different patrol assignment in a different part of the city with a whole new squad, that fear of the unknown would return to some degree. It wasn't because I didn't know my job or that I wasn't good at it. It was just because it was in a new place surrounded by new people, and that can be messy. Every work environment has its own unspoken culture, and if one either knowingly or unknowingly violates the mores and edicts of that culture, then that can lead to all sorts of problems up to outright hostility.

In the above verse from Genesis 46:3, God is speaking to Jacob (now named Israel) after he has learned that his son Joseph is alive and is the second most powerful man in Egypt behind only Pharaoh himself. The Promised Land is in the midst of a long drought, and only Egypt, under the leadership of Joseph, has adequate food. Joseph has invited his entire family to come live in Egypt so that they can be provided for but think of it from Jacob's view. His grandfather Abraham had come to this land and had prospered under God's promise. So to had his father Isaac and up until this drought, so had he. This was really the only home he had ever known. To exacerbate the situation, he was the head of a clan that included eleven sons and their wives and children, plus livestock and possessions. According to Genesis 46:26, that totaled to sixty-six people that he, as head of the family, was responsible for. In the midst of what I'm sure was some serious internal questioning, God told him to not be afraid to make the move to Egypt and then gave him three promises: that he (i.e., his family) would become a great nation while in the land of Egypt, that God would eventually bring Jacob's family back out of Egypt, and finally that he would die peacefully in Egypt, with Joseph there to take care of him. I love the phrase in the Bible for that last promise—"*Joseph will put his hand on your eyes.*" It reminds me of every old movie and TV show when someone dies and then another person reaches over and shuts their eyes before they pull a sheet or blanket over the dead guy.

God tells us also to not be afraid when He is moving us about. In fact, when we are really submitting to God's will, I think it should be something that we expect. The last earthly command from Jesus was to "*go therefore and make disciples of all the nations*: (Matthew 28:19). That is an impossible command to fully carry out if we stay rooted in one place. So don't be afraid when you have to change things up in your life. I know that none of us like our carefully crafted lives thrown into chaos (our view by the way, not God's), but like with Jacob, there's a perfect plan already in place.

One of my favorite verses, and the verse that we had inscribed on my daughter Chelsea's tombstone, is Jeremiah 29:11: "'*For I know the plans I have for you'—this is the LORD's declaration—'plans for your welfare, not for disaster, to give you a future and a hope.'*" When we really believe this, then the fear of going someplace new ceases to exist.

*   *   *   *   *

Moses hid his face because he was afraid to
look at God. (Exodus 3:6b)

There are a lot of funny memes and GIFs around usually featuring pets or very young children who have done something wrong and now will not look at the person who has discovered the deed, which is oftentimes blatantly strewn about the room. But as adults, we can also experience that same fear. Depending on who my supervisor was at that time, there was nothing more nerve-racking than to get a message from my sergeant that he or she wanted to see me. The same knot in the pit of my stomach would also manifest itself when I was a sergeant, and my lieutenant would ask to see me in the middle of my shift. But I've subsequently learned that this is common to almost everyone unless you are the ultimate top dog. Lieutenants feel it when their commander contacts them. And commanders feel that same uneasiness when their assistant chief suddenly shows up in their office. When your boss suddenly wants to talk to you—while it can be good, bad, or indifferent—fear often takes us to the worst possible scenario. Of course, it's even worse when you know you have done something that is either flat-out wrong or even just not quite as right as it should have been.

When I was about nineteen years old, I went to a party where I had way too many tequila sunrises (it was the '70s, so that was a popular drink). Somehow, I made it home and passed out in my room. Now my room was very '70s modern with its large white area rug, black beanbag chair and black-light wall posters. Sometime in the night, my stomach rejected a large amount of its contents onto the aforementioned white carpet. Tequila sunrises are made with, among other ingredients, grenadine, which is a very sweet and a very red syrup. So when my mother came in to invite me to join the family for breakfast, the evidence of what I had been involved in the night before was evident both by sight and by smell. I did not want to see my mother's face because I knew the disappointment and hurt that I had caused her, not to mention the destruction of my carpet. But then she spoke, just seven little words that destroyed me: "Your body knows when it's been poisoned." And then she left my doorway and went back to the kitchen to see to my younger brothers. I couldn't look at her for the rest of the day because I knew what I had done, but even then, she nursed me through the worst hangover of my life.

The verse from Exodus 3:6 comes from the story of Moses and the burning bush. At this point in his life, he had been raised by the Pharaoh's daughter as a prince of Egypt. He had committed murder of an Egyptian and had fled to the desert where he had gotten married and became a shepherd for his father-in-law. He had been in the desert, according to Acts 7:30, for forty years when God spoke to him and told him to remove his shoes because he's standing on holy ground. Then when God identified Himself, Moses hid his face because he's afraid to look at a holy God. Moses saw God's power and magnificence in just a bush that was on fire and yet not being burned up and immediately realized what kind of a man he was and had been. He immediately knew that his relationship to the God of his ancestors was not what it should be. But God never addressed it! Instead, He told Moses that He had seen how the Israelites have been abused by the Egyptians and that He wanted Moses, a former murderer hiding in the desert, to go back before the Pharaoh and lead his people out. So while Moses accurately saw himself for what he was, God saw him for who he was going to be under God's direction.

I know that I've done this face hiding thing from God on several occasions. I messed up big time, and then instead of going to a loving and merciful God, I act like a freaked out four-year-old and just don't look at Him. For me anyway, I think that it's equal parts shame and not wanting to see that hurt that I've caused. I've even done the really dumb move of becoming mad at God over my own self-centered decisions. Again, like a petulant child, I just won't look at him. But this makes me really glad that I serve a patient and merciful God who sees the person that He is making me into, a person who will one day be conformed to the image of His own son Jesus. The really good news is that He is doing it all because if it was left up to me, I would have failed out of the program a long time ago.

Let me fast-forward you, then, a few years into the life of Moses. He and the Israelites are still camped around Mount Sinai, and Moses has set up a tent outside of the camp where he meets with God. God tells him to head for the Promised Land, and in Exodus 33:11 it reads, "*The LORD spoke with Moses face to face, just as a man speaks with his friend.*" Now we also know from Scripture that he did not see God's face because God had already told him that no one can see His face and live. When Moses had asked to see God's glory, God had told him that He would put him in a crevice in the rock and pass by but that He would cover Moses with His hand as He did so and that after He had passed, Moses could see His back. That's as close as anyone has come. But notice how Moses and God are interacting. It's like two friends who talk face-to-face and look each other right in the eye. That's an impressive turnaround for the guy who is originally afraid to even look at a manifestation of God in a burning bush.

Have you ever done this on a human scale? You know, done something wrong to someone so that you can't or won't look them in the face? Maybe you have tried to go back and apologize later, but they either did not accept your admitting what you did or say they did but then keep bringing it back up and hanging it over your head so that you know they really didn't forgive you. Now you're afraid to see them or interact with them. So let's have some more fear-dispelling good news. God isn't like that! The Bible tells us in 1 John 1:9, *"If we confess our sins, He is faithful and righteous to forgive us our sins and to cleanse us from all unrighteousness."* Then, like Moses, He talks to us face-to-face like a person speaks to their friend. That's some pretty amazing stuff. I don't ever have to be afraid to look at God.

*   *   *   *   *

But Moses said to the people, "Don't be afraid. Stand firm and see the LORD's salvation He will provide for you today; for the Egyptians you see today, you will never see again." (Exodus 14:13)

It is one thing to say to yourself that you won't be afraid, but it is quite something else to just stand still when something is coming at you that you know is dangerous and deadly. Perhaps one of the greatest visual representations of that is the famous picture of the lone student facing down a line of tanks in the Tiananmen Square protests of 1989. Those massive machines have only one function: to kill and destroy. Even without the incredible firepower that each tank is equipped with, just its size and ability to move was enough to crush that lone protestor, and yet there he stood, and the photograph of that moment has come to symbolize the fearlessness of a lone individual in the face of overwhelming power.

As a police officer, I often had to stand my ground, but I have to admit that it was never, at least to my knowledge at the time, against undefeatable power. There were times of danger, of course, like the time that I went in foot pursuit of a gangster that had just robbed a local convenience store that night. It was winter, so I had my coat on that covered my gun belt. This meant that getting to the things that I carried on my belt (gun, handcuffs, and pepper spray) took longer to access. After a short chase, the young man realized that he wasn't going to outrun me, and so he suddenly stopped and turned to face me. The chase had gone down a major thoroughfare, and so the scene was fairly well lit up. This allowed me to see the handle of a pistol sticking up from the waistband of his pants. I stopped as well, and we were now about five yards apart. And then I opted to do what I had seen in a number of western movies instead of good police procedure. I reached behind me with my left hand and pulled my coat back to reveal my Glock 9mm pistol on my right hip. I then moved my right hand to just above the gun and told this young would-be robber to "try it." It wasn't high noon, and I was no fast draw expert, and to this day, I cannot tell you why I did this. But now we stood there just facing each other with the possibility of death or serious injury hanging heavy in the air between us. About that time, I realized what a stupid position I had put us both in, but now here it was, and I had to stand firm. After what seemed like a minute or two (but was really probably only seconds), as the gangster considered his options, he suddenly said, "Okay, okay," and he slowly put both hands in the air. I then ordered him to his knees and put out my location so that the other responding officers could find us and assist me with taking him into custody.

In police work, we always try to put the odds in our favor whenever possible, either through sheer numbers, various debilitating options (Tasers, pepper spray, etc.), personal protection devices (ballistic shields, helmets, bulletproof vests), or superior firepower. This does tend to make standing firm in the face of danger and death a lot easier to do even when everything inside you is telling you to either run away or to seek shelter from whatever you are facing. For the Israelites, though, they did not have those options. Even the sheer numbers option didn't come into play as a lot of the people were women, children, and men who had passed the age of being able to fight. But like that lone student in Tiananmen Square, God told them to not be afraid and to show it by standing firm and watch as He handled what was arguably one of the most feared militaries of its time.

To put the verse into context, it is after the plagues and everyone in Egypt who did not have the blood of the Passover lamb on their doorway had suffered the death of their firstborn child along with the death of the firstborn of all their animals (Genesis 11:5). To say the country was devastated is probably too mild of a term. But now, finally, the Pharaoh agreed to let the Israelites go, and not only did they just leave, but they had also previously requested gold, silver, and clothing from their Egyptian neighbors who now willingly gave it to them. Thus, as the Bible puts it, they plundered the Egyptians (Genesis 12:36). But now here they were, six hundred thousand men plus women and children and all their flocks and herds in the wilderness, and they had come up against the Red Sea. Now to be fair, we don't know where along the roughly 1,400-mile-long seawater inlet that this happened. We do know, though, that the average depth for the Red Sea is about 1,608 feet deep and that at its maximum width, it is around 221 miles wide.[16] And we do know that they did not have any boats. So now with an impossible barrier to the east, one of the greatest militaries of its time was coming from the west with the intention of bringing them back into slavery and to recover their country's wealth and in the face of all this, God told them to not be afraid and to stand firm.

Now as great as Charlton Heston was as Moses, the movie got it wrong. God did not part the Red Sea in seconds and everybody just hurried across. The standing firm thing took quite a bit longer. If you know your Bible history, the angel of the Lord led the people as a pillar of smoke by day and a pillar of fire by night, but on this occasion, he moved to the rear and protected them. Plus, the Egyptians didn't just go charging in. This was a lot of people after all, and not only that, they were also a valuable commodity. So they set up camp, perhaps so that they could decide just how best to retake this massive group of people.

The Bible tells us that "the cloud was there in the darkness, yet it lit up the night. So neither group came near the other all night long" (Exodus 14:20). It was after God moved to protect them that Moses did as he had been instructed and stretched out his hand over the sea. God then sent what was called a strong east wind that blew all night.

[16.] All the Red Sea statistics are from *Encyclopedia Britannica*, accessed September 26, 2017, at https://www.britannica.com/place/Red-Sea.

By the next day then, the sea was parted and the ground was dry and the people were able to cross. But here is where we are missing some more facts. We don't know if this was a narrow path (like the movie and most Sunday school pictures), which would require this massive group of people hours to all make the crossing or, if it was a really wide opening, which would really shorten the amount of time it took all those people and animals to cross. The only thing that we do know is that there was a wall of water somewhere in the neighborhood of 1,600 feet (or about 150 feet higher than the Empire State building) to the north and south of them that was just suspended there. But the point is that the people had to stand firm all night and, to some point, the next day before they were able to make the crossing with "only" the angel of the Lord as a pillar of smoke protecting them. They were not to panic and run or were they to give up and just go back and take their punishment for having the temerity to just up and leave their masters. They were to stay in place while God caused this all-night wind to set up His receiving honor from the Egyptians and the protection of His people.

I have to wonder what that night was like. My mind at least would have been racing, and I don't know how much sleep I would have had. Experiencing this wind coming across the water must have been incredible. I would have seen the pillar to the west and known that somewhere behind it was a military with all the latest gear and weapons meaning to drag me and my family back. And then I was told that I was not supposed to be afraid, and I was to demonstrate that by standing firm where I was. This was to really be faith in action.

The people obeyed and then crossed on dry land, but God wasn't done dealing with the Egyptians, and again, we need to see what the Bible says and stay away from movie descriptions and well-meaning artist renditions. God allows them to go into pursuit once again with their swift-moving chariots, but in Exodus 14:24–25, it says that "*the LORD looked down on the Egyptian forces from the pillar of fire and cloud, and threw them into confusion. He caused their chariot wheels to swerve and made them drive with difficulty.*" Moses doesn't tell us how God did this, but he directed the psalmist Asaph to give us a glimpse in Psalm 77:16–20. In Psalm 77, we see the description of a sudden and very intense thunderstorm complete with lightning and thunder and earthquake and what is described as a whirlwind. There are four words that our English translations use the term *whirlwind*, and they describe it as any windstorm that is destructive.[17] This particular term in Hebrew is *galgal*.[18] And it is only here in Psalm 77:18 that we find this particular word with its designation of a circular motion.

While Cecil B. DeMille did give us a really good movie, he totally sold short just what God did to the pursuing army of the Egyptians in the seabed of the Red sea. God again used natural phenomena to stop the mightiest army of its day right where He wanted them stopped. The interesting thing, too, was that right before God destroyed them, they realized just who they are up against (apparently, after all those plagues they were kind of slow learners). Exodus 14:25 recorded them as saying "'*Let's get away from Israel,' the Egyptians said, 'because Yahweh is fighting for them against Egypt!*'" Now either Moses was supernaturally told what they were saying or someone, Moses probably, was close enough to have heard it. Think about that. In the midst of all that storm activity, they were heard to say that they need to "get out of here" because they've finally realized that it was God Himself who was fighting for the Israelites. So either they were really loud or they got within shouting distance before God slammed the door shut on them. It was then when they finally realized the folly of their actions that God authorized Moses to again stretch out his hand over the sea, and it returned to its former place as the Egyptians were fleeing back toward the western shoreline, killing them all. So to sum it up, the entire Israelite nation had to decide to not be afraid and to stand firm all night and then to cross through a dry seabed that shouldn't be there. Then Moses had to remain standing firm, this time on the eastern shoreline, as the Egyptians came across after them. He remained firm as they get within shouting distance until

---

[17.] Trent C. Butler (general editor), *Holman Bible Dictionary* (Nashville, TN: Holman Bible Publishers, 1991), 1,408.

[18.] Strong's 1534.

God stopped them cold with an incredible array of natural phenomena. This is what trusting God really looks like up close and personal.

God gives us the same directive over and over throughout the Bible: Don't be afraid. Stand firm where He has placed you and watch Him work so that He gets the glory. But what is our usual response? Make and initiate plans of our own design. Run and hide to avoid uncomfortable or even dangerous situations. Freak out when the enemy gets within shouting distance and give up our ground. It takes faith to not be afraid and to stand firm real faith, but the reward is always victory and God getting the glory.

* * * * *

Therefore, don't be afraid of them, since there is nothing covered that won't be uncovered and nothing hidden that won't be made known. (Matthew 10:26)

Because of my profession I have been called a lot of things. Some of them positive and flattering like hero and guardian angel, but a lot of them have been words and phrases that are more commonly found on seedy bathroom stalls and are usually reserved for something or someone that is despised and detested above all else. Neither of these got to me to any great extent, although the less flattering terms did seem to rankle a number of my coworkers. In the operations orders of my department, there are directives that require us to maintain our public communication on a very professional level. We are not supposed to sound like and conduct ourselves in the same vulgar manner that we experience as a part of our daily fare. But law enforcement is made up of fallible people who make mistakes and occasionally forget that little life lesson that we are supposed to have learned when we were young. You know, the one that says just because the other person is doing it doesn't mean that you have to do it as well.

One of our hallmarks, the thing that is supposed to separate my profession from everyone else, is our integrity. As a sergeant, one of the things that I have always stressed to my officers is to tell the unfiltered truth especially when they have messed up. I told them that messing up is going to happen and that while there may be some discipline involved, depending upon the severity of the issue, almost anything is survivable if they will just tell the truth. The facts have an interesting way of coming to the surface eventually, and if they have told the truth, then they have nothing to fear when all the facts of an incident do become known. But again, because my profession is made up of fallible people, occasionally someone will think that they can outsmart the system and bury or hide the truth. In this day and age with just about everyone having a cell phone that can record both photographs and sound, the old days of having an unbreakable "He said—she said" tie about the facts of a matter have become much less likely. Someone always seems to have taken a picture or recorded a conversation, and that makes checking the veracity of a statement much, much easier. One of my officers got caught on the short end of this.

As a field supervisor, getting phone calls or a request to see me from unhappy citizens was a common part of the job. The complaints ranged from just a perceived general poor attitude to claims of malfeasance and even criminal conduct. I am happy to report, at least in my experience, that the vast majority of these were either just a misunderstanding, an exaggeration of the facts, or just a downright lie that was easily exposed. But occasionally, I would get one that seemed legitimate, and I would have to investigate to find out the truth of the matter. In one particular case, my officer and a motorist had gotten into a verbal exchange over the reasons for a traffic stop. After the initial contact, the driver had turned on the voice-recording feature of his cell phone prior to the officer returning with his citation. Upon my officer returning, the driver immediately launched into another round of questioning both the law and the officer's view while maintaining that he had not violated any of the traffic laws that he was accused of in the citation. This was where my officer failed to maintain his composure, and instead of just calmly restating what the violations were and how the driver could address them, he delved into a curse-word laden back-and-forth with the driver that ended with the driver refusing to sign the citation, whereupon he was promptly taken into custody and placed in the back of the officer's patrol car.

Now I need to explain that in Arizona at least, most traffic violations are civil in nature. That means they are not criminal conduct, and therefore, no arrest can be made. The procedure when a driver elects not to sign a citation is to explain (and the wording is actually printed on the citation) that by signing, they are not admitting anything but they are merely acknowledging that they have received a copy. If they still refuse to sign, then the officer merely writes "Served" on the signature line and gives the driver his copies and allows them to leave. But of course, that wasn't what happened.

At that point, the officer realized that there was a problem and called me to the scene. He explained what had happened but left out a few important details while embellishing others that had caused him to take the driver into custody. I quickly figured out that the driver needed to be released and directed the officer to do so. Upon exiting the patrol car, the driver said that he wanted to tell me his side of the story, and while most of it matched up with what my officer had said, there were some glaring differences as well. I told the driver that there were differences in the story but that I wasn't there, so I could not believe one side over the other. That's when he told me that he had recorded the second half of the contact and offered to let me listen to it. Before he even turned on the playback feature, I could see that this was a person who was actually holding the winning hand and not someone trying to pull off a gutsy bluff. With the truth of the matter now playing clearly in my ear, I could accurately ascertain exactly what had happened and how it had come to be, so I thanked the driver and released him to go on about his business while I got to deal with my officer. *There is nothing hidden that won't be made known.*

In the verse from Matthew 10:26, Jesus is talking to His disciples and letting them know how things were going to be. It actually starts back in verse 24 when He tells them that disciples are not better than their teacher. If something happens to the teacher, then the disciples should expect the same. He then refers to being called Beelzebub. This may refer to the soon-coming time when He casts out a demon and then the religious leaders of His day said that He was doing it under the authority of Beelzebub, the ruler of demons (Matthew 12:24). And it is because of this truth that disciples are not better than their teacher but that they do not need to be afraid because He assured them that no truth will remain hidden permanently and that lies and evil motives will eventually be revealed for what they are.

I have seen a lot of this, even gone there myself on occasion—the fear-based lie or attempted cover-up. And you would think that as a rational and functional person, I would learn that while this occasionally works in the short run, it is never a permanent solution. And when that which is covered up is uncovered, the resulting issue is far greater than what I would have faced had I just addressed the issue truthfully at the time. But fear has a way of almost instantly moving us away from our rational thought into a dark void that we want instant release from. And whether it's with intentional forethought or just fear-based lying (the Bible doesn't differentiate), the Bible has a lot to say about lying. It is one of the Ten Commandments in the Old Testament, and it is linked with cowards, unbelievers, vile murderers, sexually immoral, sorcerers, and idolaters who will share in "the lake that burns with fire and sulfur" (Revelation 21:8) in the New Testament. God's opinion about lying, *any lying*, is pretty strong and definite. As disciples of Jesus, we should not be afraid as that can lead to panic-lying but have the faith that what is true will be uncovered and that hidden evil will be made known.

*　　*　　*　　*　　*

He will not fear bad news; his heart is confident, trusting in the LORD. (Psalm 112:7)

One of the worst assignments that an officer has to carry out is making death notifications to the next of kin because you never know how the reaction is going to be and as an officer you have no or very limited resources to deal with the situation. Oftentimes, for me anyway, the situation went something like this: A person died somewhere else in the country, and that jurisdiction contacted my department with the name and address of the person to be notified. Then I would get dispatched with nothing more than the dead person's name, who I was to contact, and the contact information for the local authorities to give to the next of kin. So now I headed into a potentially emotional and volatile situation not knowing anything.

My head is full of questions that experience tells me that the person whom I deliver this news to may ask me: "I would like to know was the death unexpected and if it was, was it an accident?" or "Was it suicide or homicide?" If it was from so-called natural causes, was it so sudden that the deceased didn't have time to contact his or her family? Then the next round of questions pops in: How do I deal with the reaction of the person that I am making this notification to? Is there anything that I can do to assist them? But instead, I take my limited information and ring the doorbell. Sometimes, the information is received with a sense of relief or expectation, but all too often, there is initial shock followed by an outpouring of grief that in some instances was so intense that I had some concern for the person's well-being. But having no answers for either their pain or the nature of the circumstances, I gave my condolences, and I returned to my patrol car, made a note in my log, and waited for my next call for service while another tiny cut to my soul is being filled in with scar tissue.

But of course, being human, I also have had to receive bad news. And like all of you, I can point to any number of them, but for me, the worst came in the spring of 1989. My wife and I had recently learned that we were expecting our third child. We had two healthy girls, and nothing indicated that this was anything but a normal pregnancy until we went in for an ultrasound. The tech did a good job of remaining professional, but my wife picked up on her reactions and knew that something was wrong. We went home, and in a very short time, her doctor called and told us that our baby had a condition called anencephaly. This meant that our child was missing a large portion of her head and brain. But what hit me, and I still remember it to this day, was the doctor's statement: "The baby's condition is not compatible with life." Wow, talk about bad news;

this was impossible news. In a time before the internet, we quickly scrounged around to find everything we could about this condition, and what we learned wasn't good. Then we had to decide how we were going to handle the situation. The doctor's suggestion was to terminate the pregnancy in that there was no viable outcome, but my wife and I both believe that elective abortion is murder. The problem is that until we got to this point in our lives, we had never had to put our belief into practical practice. So after a lot of crying, praying, and talking, we decided that since God had allowed this in our lives, we would go through it with His help, just like any other pregnancy until it was over.

Everything else went quite normally over the next months. We learned the baby was a girl and named her Chelsea. She continued to grow and move around in my wife's belly. My wife and I "spoke" to her just like we had done with her two older sisters. But then it came time for the delivery. Chelsea had not died in utero as it often happens with babies with this condition. To complicate matters a bit more, my wife had to have cesarean birthing experiences, so we had to schedule Chelsea's birth, knowing that it would also mean the end of her short life. We knew that it would be traumatic for everyone involved, so the hospital staff was warned, and we handpicked every-one who would be a part of the operation so that they knew ahead of time what they were going to be involved in. On November 10, 1989, a beautiful baby girl was born, Chelsea Elisabeth Sexton, who just happened to be missing most of the top and back of her head. In God's gracious timing, she lived for about forty-five minutes. Just long enough for her mother to hold her and for her to wet down the front of my scrubs (completing a perfect track record for all six of our kids to get me at one time or another).

Of course, there was a lot of questioning as to why this had happened and would it happen again. Why us? But the answer didn't come for several years. Then one day, a person from our church con-tacted my wife and said that she knew of a young gal who had just found out that her child had anencephaly and if my wife would be willing to talk with her. My wife readily agreed and helped to walk that young lady through her own version of this trauma. This scenario was repeated several times over the new few years including one in another country that my wife then corresponded with to help her through the issue. Again, and I know I'm dating myself, but this was before the instant global communication that we enjoy today. So now we knew that Chelsea's life had a meaning (as everyone's life does), and it was to prepare us, my wife especially, to help others who were facing the same kind of issue and, for Christians, the tough choices that come along with it.

Psalms 112, which starts this section, gives a description of the traits of a righteous person. It is an acrostic poem in the original Hebrew that is a companion with Psalms 111.[19] It opens and expands on the last verse of Psalm 111, which says, "*The fear of the Lord is the beginning of wisdom; all who follow His instructions have good insight. His praise endures forever.*" The opening line of 112 is "*Hallelujah! Happy is the man who fears the Lord, taking great delight in His commandments.*" So this fear is that reverential awe that I wrote about earlier. But then down in verse 7, we read that a characteristic of a righteous person is that they will not fear bad news. How is that even possible, you may ask? I know that I did when I read it because it seems that in this day and age, there is almost nothing but bad news that seems designed to make fear the only reasonable response. But then I remembered the words of Paul when he wrote to his young protégé Timothy about the suffering that he was going through in 2 Timothy 1:11–12: "*For this gospel I was appointed a herald, apostle, and teacher, and that is why I suffer these things. But I am not ashamed; because I know the One I have believed in and am persuaded that He is able to guard what has been entrusted to me until that day.*" The reality, at least for a Christian, is that there isn't any bad news that is permanent. All bad news is temporary at best and may actually be for later good, like the day my wife and I found out about Chelsea. Now that's not to say that I'm a Pollyanna (from a 1913 novel of the same name by Eleanor H. Porter about a young girl that is excessively cheerful and optimistic) and not concerned when I hear about nations like

---

[19.] https://www.biblestudytools.com/commentaries/jamieson-fausset-brown/psalms-76-150/psalms-112.html.

Iran and North Korea that threaten the world's stability. And I was really upset the day that the doctors came in and told my mother and me that she was terminal. But what I do know is that God's control is complete and that absolutely nothing can touch me without His permission. No gangster's bullet or knife will ever touch me unless God allows it. The same goes for any nuclear missile, whether it is under the control of a sane leader or an insane one. The death of a loved one or the loss of finances or anything else you care to name. My faith is in the promised future held in place by the God who created the universe and does not change or waver. With God, all bad news is temporary!

I really like the quote by Bishop Robert Leighton as he commented on this psalm. He wrote about the righteous person that "his heart is fixed, or prepared, ready, and in arms for all services; resolved not to give back, able to meet all adventures, and stand its ground. God is unchangeable; and therefore faith is invincible, for it sets the heart on him; fastens it there on the rock of eternity; then let winds blow and storms arise, it cares not."[20] Don't read this wrong. It's not that I, as a Christian, am uncaring about bad news. I'm human, and that's just not true. It's that after I get over the initial shock of the matter, my faith takes me back to the unchangeable nature of God. If He can't be moved, then neither should I be able to be freaked out about bad news. In fact, like the psalmist writes, I am confident that God has got this, and no matter what the short-term results are (as devastating as they might me in the here and now), the long-term results are that I will be with Him and everything will be all right.

[20.] https://www.biblestudytools.com/commentaries/treasury-of-david/psalms-112-7.html.

APRIL

> In the morning you shall say, Would God
> it were evening! and at evening you shall say,
> Would God it were morning! because of the
> fear of your heart by which you shall fear, and
> because of the sight of your eyes which you shall
> see. (Deuteronomy 28:67 KJV 2000 Bible)

The word translated as fear in this passage is one of the other Hebrew words that have, until recently, been translated into the English word *fear*. The Hebrew word is *pachad*[21] and means an (sudden) alarm or the feeling that something horrible is about to happen. The idea here is to dread something that is coming. Thus, *Holman* translates the verse like this: "*In the morning you will say, 'If only it were evening!' and in the evening you will say, 'If only it were morning!'—because of the dread you will have in your heart and because of what you will see.*"

Let me put the verse into context for you. God is warning the Israelites (back in verse 58 of the same chapter) that if they are not careful to obey the law by fearing (i.e., the awe and reverence that is due God) the awe-inspiring name of the Lord, your God, He would bring the plagues of Egypt on them and remove His hand of blessing. The result would be that they would have *a trembling heart, failing eyes, and a despondent spirit* (Deuteronomy 28:65). Knowing what is coming, God tells them that they will react with dread and wishing that they were anywhere but where they would find themselves if they disobey.

---

21. Strong's 6343.

On a different level, I know that we all experience dread at times. When we were children, it might have been from a statement, something like "Wait until your father comes home and hears about this!" or when report cards were sent home and you knew that you had failed to achieve an adequate grade and had no one to blame but yourself. Later in life, it can come from things like suddenly being called into your boss's office when you were not expecting to hear from him or her and especially if something has just gone wrong. You begin to instantly dread having to face them and the possible consequences. As an officer, I hated receiving a message that my sergeant wanted to see me. As I drove to the designated meeting spot, I would go over every call that I had been on that day carefully rehearsing what had happened, what I had said (or didn't say) and why, and what the outcome had been. Of course, as often as not, my sergeant just needed to give me something like a subpoena or let me know some information that had just come out. But there were times that he had received a call from an unhappy citizen and was trying to find out from me if their complaint was valid.

When I got my stripes, I remembered that sense of dread, so I usually tried to let my officers know why I wanted to see them along with the request to meet me. But the lieutenants that I reported to rarely, if ever, thought to do the same, and so when I would be asked to meet them, I was right back in the dread box. The problem now was that I wasn't only going over everything that I had done but also everything that my squad had been involved with as well, which is a much bigger load to have to answer for. Of course, dread can come from other sources as well, things like knowing that the monthly bills are coming due and that there will not be enough in the bank account to cover them. Or perhaps it is a medical diagnosis such as cancer with the possible radiation and chemotherapy treatments and how they may affect you. The thing about dread is that at its core, it is an extreme fear of the unknown, almost to the point of terror.

The keyword here for me is the first word of Deuteronomy 28:58, which is the word *if.* So much of our dread has me looking backward and thinking that if I hadn't done (or said) something or if I had done (or said) something, then I wouldn't be facing the impending consequences that are looming before me. Sometimes, it is forward-looking, but those thoughts begin with the word *if* as well. Thoughts like "If I could only…" run to the forefront of our thinking with the resulting dread that we won't be able to actually accomplish the "if only" thoughts. I cannot change any of the ifs of my past, but I can endeavor to avoid the negative ifs of my future. For the most part, avoiding the negative ifs of my future means being obedient to what I know to be the right thing to do. When I am carefully following the laws of my country, state, city, and employer, I mitigate the amount of possible negative outcomes that I might encounter. I find that I get called into an unplanned meeting a whole lot less when I'm doing what I'm supposed to be doing the way that I'm supposed to be doing it. The same holds true for my obedience to the directives of God. While God doesn't call me in for an impromptu meeting, as a loving Father, He does give me the discipline that I need to get my undivided attention.

The Israelites were warned not only what would happen to them as a people *if* they failed to obey the law and obey it in the right way, but they were also even told how they would react to the resulting consequences of their disobedience. They were told that the consequences would be so severe that they would doubt that they would even survive and that they would long for the next day or evening because they were so afraid that they would not survive the time of day they were in. So by being obedient, I can mitigate, if not outright eliminate, the negative ifs in my future, which only leaves me with those that I have no control over. As a Christian (one who believes that Jesus, a member of the three-in-one God lived, died as a payment for my sins, and then rose again to the position of Lord in my life), I have the assurance in the simple and yet profound statement from Romans 8:31: "*What then are we to say about these things? If God is for us, who is against us?*" I no longer have anything to dread even if it is something as awful as a diagnosis of a disease that will have terrible effects that will ultimately kill me. While I understand that they won't be pleasant and that even Jesus himself—as He faced the impending trial, beatings, crucifixion, and ultimately the separation caused by His taking on the sin of all mankind for all time—prayed that *if possible*,[22] He would not have to drink from that cup. I know the promise that God has for me in Romans 8:28: "*We know that all things work together for the good of those who love God: those who are called according to His purpose.*" So while I may very well dread the temporary pain and discomfort that I may have to endure, the ultimate outcome is going to be good for me!

Proverbs 1:26–31 spells out the reaction, though, for those of us who think that they can do it on their own. Those people who think that they do not need or want God's wisdom and control in their lives. God's reaction here should bring dread because those verses read

> I, in turn, will laugh at your calamity. I will mock when terror strikes you, when terror strikes you like a storm and your calamity comes like a whirlwind, when trouble and stress overcome you. Then they will call me, but I won't answer; they will search for me, but won't find me. Because they hated knowledge, didn't choose to fear the LORD, were not interested in my counsel, and rejected all my correction, they will eat the fruit of their way and be glutted with their own schemes.

*   *   *   *   *

> So don't be afraid therefore; you are worth more than many sparrows." (Matthew 10:31)

One of the big topics in our schools over the last couple of decades has been the topic of self-esteem. It was thought to be the panacea that would miraculously raise the academic performance of every student by feeding them a never-ending stream of positive affirmations. Everything, no matter how inconsequential, seemingly

---

22. Matthew 26:39.

had an award attached to it; and thus, the participation trophy, the target of many a comedian's wit, came into existence. Empty praise for what even children realized were meaningless things of course did not work, and the tide has begun to ebb in favor of language and communication that will encourage children to realize that they made a mistake and to work through it and to not fear tackling even harder work. This is the old "Get back on the horse that just threw you" way of thinking.

In an article by Michael Alison Chandler in the *Washington Post* on January 15, 2012,[23] she noted that "a growing body of research over three decades shows that easy, unearned praise does not help students but instead interferes with significant learning opportunities." The article goes on to point out that the new concepts center on words like *persistence, risk-taking,* and *resilience* are amazingly akin to those ideas on how to mold a successful student that were in place for the grandparents and great grandparents of a modern-day grade school student. This reversal in thinking again proves the old and oft quoted maxim "Everything old is new again."

The verse from Matthew 10 that heads this section comes from a long set of instructions and teaching that Jesus gave to the twelve as He was sending them out to begin their work. Verses 26–31 have to do with fearing (the awe-based respect for) God. It comes on the heels of a long passage that tells the disciples that they will be persecuted just as He would be. In what is perhaps one of the greatest "Don't fear" quotes of Jesus, He tells these men in verse 28: "*Don't fear those who kill the body but are not able to kill the soul; rather, fear Him who is able to destroy both soul and body in hell.*" So first off, get your priorities straight and focus on the real power. But then He tells them just how benevolent God and His powers are with an illustration about sparrows. Jesus points out that sparrows are not particularly valuable ("two for a penny," verse 29) but that "*not one of them falls to the ground without your Father's consent.*" When you stop

---

23. https://www.washingtonpost.com/local/education/in-schools-self-esteem-boosting-is-losing-favor-to-rigor-finer-tuned-praise/2012/01/11/gIQAXFnF1P_story.html?utm_term=.717c566ae618.

to think about it, that is an amazing statement. Think about how many sparrows (not to mention all the other bird species) there are around the planet at any given time. Various scientific websites postulate that the number is in the billions, and yet Jesus says that not one of them dies (falls to the ground) without God's consent! Then He makes it personal for these men in verse 30 as He tells them that *"even the hairs of your head have all been counted."* Essentially, Jesus told them that God knows what is going on with every aspect of His creation, but He knows them personally as well. Then He concludes that section with the greatest basis for self-esteem of all time as He told them that they were worth more than many sparrows that God watched over.

My personal self-esteem has waxed and waned over the years, as I based it on what others recognized me for. We are all susceptible to this to one degree or another, which is why flattery often works so well on us. Over the course of my career, I was fortunate enough to have received a number of commendations and the occasional plaque to commemorate something that went particularly well. Since I began writing this book, I have retired from the Phoenix Police Department, and now all those plaques and commendations have been unceremoniously regulated to an unmarked box in the garage. One day that box and its contents will no doubt become property of the city dump, but my self-esteem will not go with it. My self-esteem is now based upon how God sees me, and it is personal. He knows the hair count on my head (a number that is decreasing I'm afraid), and He says that I'm an important part of His creation! Even though there are billions of sparrows around the globe that He cares for, He tells me that He knows me personally and that I'm worth more than a whole lot of sparrows. Talk about self-esteem. How can I not look in the mirror each morning and think that I'm important because God does? And that is in spite of all the dumb and disobedient things that I am going to do that day.

It also addresses any fear that I may have throughout the day. Notice that Jesus did not just say that God was aware when a sparrow fell but that it did not occur without God's *consent.* If He does not give the consent for that being the exact time and place for that individual sparrow to die, it does not happen! And Jesus told those disciples that they were of more value than a whole flock of sparrows. I do not have anything to fear because nothing can happen to me without God's consent. Now combine that with Romans 8:28, which we looked at in the last section. If God gives His consent, then ultimately, if I love God and am called according to His purpose, whatever He gives His consent for will be for my good. Wow, I can feel my self-esteem rising while I'm writing this. If God thinks that I'm that kind of important, then I will as well.

*   *   *   *   *

> Now Absalom commanded his young men, "Watch Amnon until he is in a good mood from the wine. When I order you to strike Amnon, then kill him. Don't be afraid. Am I not the one who has commanded you? Be strong and courageous!" (2 Samuel 13:28)

This is going to be a different look into fear. This time, we will look at the fear of doing something that we know to be or at least suspect is wrong but we are then encouraged by someone else to go ahead and do it. It can be especially compelling if that other person is willing to take the fallout or be responsible for your actions. For those of you who are not familiar with the story, let me give you the condensed version. Absalom and Amnon were half brothers and sons of King David. Amnon was the oldest son and was the heir apparent to David's throne. Amnon was probably best known for having raped his half sister Tamar, who was the daughter of David and Maachah. In spite of the Mosaic Law against having sexual relations between half brothers and sisters, Amnon felt an overwhelming desire to have her. He then took the advice from his cousin Jonadab the son of Shimeah, David's brother, to lure Tamar into his house by pretending to be sick and getting his father to ask her to cook a special meal for him. He ignored her protests and raped her, then became disgusted with her and had her removed from his house. While David was angry about the incident, he did not elect to punish his eldest son. Absalom, Amnon's half brother and Tamar's full brother, though, held on to a very bitter grudge against Amnon for the rape of his sister and the inaction of his father. It was not until about two years later, in an act of revenge, Absalom invited all of David's sons to a feast at sheep-shearing time. He then had his servants kill Amnon after he had become intoxicated. As a result of this murder, Absalom fled to the territory of Geshur. (You can read the full story from rape to murder in 2 Samuel 13.)

What a great family—not! While I hope that most of you will look at the actions of both Amnon and Absalom with all the disgust that this story is due, I know that some of you may have experienced something not to dissimilar in your own families. While the world has become much more technologically advanced since the time of David, it seems that people and all their inherent evil continue unabated throughout recorded history. But what I want to take a closer look at is Absalom telling his servants, "Don't be afraid."

Absalom wanted his half brother killed for what he did to his full sister Tamar, but he did not apparently have the stomach to do the deed himself. Instead, he hatched a fairly elaborate plot of getting all his half brothers together for a celebration away from the palace. He then directed his servants to complete the murder at his command. Any murder itself was dangerous due to the eye-for-an-eye and tooth-for-a-tooth policy at the time. These servants, who had nothing against Amnon, could now be the recipients of a similar action at the hands of Amnon's family. Of course, in this case, it was exacerbated by the fact that this was the king's son and not just any of his sons but the eldest who would be expected to take the throne when his father died. Absalom was having them take all the risk for his own satisfaction. It is no wonder that he had to tell them to not be afraid. This type of situation, considering doing something wrong, is when fear is actually our ally. In this instance, fear is jumping up and down in our minds, screaming at us not to do something usually out of a sense of self-preservation. This type of fear takes an outside force to quell its insistence that we not do something. Or a seared conscience (1 Timothy 4:2) can also overcome that fear, but it usually takes a while to get to that kind of cold disregard. (For a quick study on a seared conscience, I recommend the website What Christians Want to Know article at https://www.whatchristianswant-toknow.com/what-is-a-seared-conscience.)

As a police officer and father, I cannot begin to count the times that I caught a bad guy or one of my kids in the midst of an act, and one of the first things out of their mouth was something akin to "He (or she) told me to do it." I do not know if that line has ever worked in the history of the world, and yet it is often the first verbal line of defense that we put out there when we get caught. And of course, with our children, we often resort to a common "dadism" (one that we probably heard when we tried the excuse) like "Well if he (or she) told you to (fill in something gross or disgusting here), would you do that?" Absalom's men knew that murder was not right, and they especially knew that murdering the king's eldest son really was not right. Absalom knew what was going on in their minds, so he told them to not be afraid because they could say they were just acting under his orders. It would be his responsibility. Of course, generally, most societies do not accept that as a viable excuse. Even more so when this type of excuse for a wrongdoing is played out on a world stage.

After WWII at the Nuremberg trials, one Nazi defendant after another tried to use the defense that he was only acting under orders. It was so often repeated that acting under the order of your superiors became knowns as the Nuremberg defense. But the German Nazi party did not invent this excuse. Peter von Hagenbach tried it as far back as 1474 and was subsequently found guilty and beheaded.[24] Of course, this is just what we know of in recorded history. It is my guess, knowing that people have not changed one iota, that at some point, Cain or Abel may have tried it on Adam and Eve when they were just boys. This type of fear, then, not wanting to do something that we know is wrong, goes to the idea that we are all born with at least a rudimentary core instinct or core knowledge of right and wrong.

---

24. Accessed on February 3, 2018, http://www.duhaime.org/LawMuseum/LawArticle-1563/1474-The-Peter-Von-Hagenbach-Trial-The-First-International-Criminal-Tribunal.aspx.

Researchers at Yale University's Infant Cognition Center, known as the Baby Lab, have come to this conclusion as well. After decades of research and tests, Paul Bloom—author of *Just Babies: The Origins of Good and Evil* and a professor of psychology at Yale—says these studies show that even before babies can speak or walk, they judge good and bad in the actions of others because they are born with a rudimentary sense of justice.[25] Of course, this agrees with the Bible's idea that mankind, upon eating the forbidden fruit, now inherently knew the difference between good and evil. Matthew 3:22 says, "*The LORD God said, 'Since man has become like one of Us, <u>knowing</u>[26] good and evil, he must not reach out, take from the tree of life, eat, and live forever.*"

Too often when we want to do something that we know is wrong, we will go in search of an Absalom in our life, a person who will tell us to not be afraid of the possible consequences and to go ahead and do what we wanted to do in the first place. We then may even seek out a Jonadab who will figure out a way for us to do it. The problem here, though, is that every time we do this or we acquiesce to another's encouragement to what we know is evil, we put a little more scar tissue on our conscience, cooking it as it is until finally, it is as tough and unusable as a charred-through piece of meat. This type of fear also often has a definite physical sign as well. In police work, we usually refer to it as the big look. Now don't overemphasize the word *big* in that phrase. It can be anything, from a sweeping of the head from side to side looking to see if someone is watching or as subtle as a quick movement of the eyes from side to side as the person is scanning for any possible threats to them completing their considered evil action. If you are a parent, I can almost guarantee that you have seen your children do this at one time or another. As a police officer, it is something we are trained to be on the lookout for. And if you have ever worked private security and monitored the surveillance cameras, you have most likely observed it hundreds if

---

[25.] Accessed on February 3, 2018, https://www.cnn.com/2014/02/12/us/baby-lab-morals-ac360/index.html.

[26.] Italics and underline added for emphasis.

not thousands of times, as it almost always immediately precedes the evil or criminal action.

So the next time that you are considering doing something evil, criminal, or just plain wrong and you feel some level of fear, do not squelch it. It is there for a reason. That is your conscience jumping up in down in your head (I picture the emotions from Pixar's 2015 movie *Inside Out*), telling you not to go ahead. And if someone else begins to tell you to not be afraid and to go ahead and do it and they are your superior, you will be in a tough place but one that you have to hold on to your morals if for no other reason than to keep you from cooking your conscience to a burnt-up useless thing.

*   *   *   *   *

The LORD is the One who will go before
you. He will be with you; He will not leave you
or forsake you. Do not be afraid or discouraged.
(Deuteronomy 31:8)

This is perhaps, at least in my way of thinking, one of the greatest promises in the Bible, and I'm not talking about the fact that God has promised to never leave us or forsake us. That is an outstanding promise that we can absolutely depend upon. What I'm talking about, though, is in the first sentence. Did you see it? God states that He will go before you. That means that when you find yourself in the midst of that devastating situation or that time of incredible blessing, God is already there! He was in the midst of the situation and waiting for you to arrive in it.

To put this verse into its biblical and historical context, the Israelites have come to the Jordan and are getting ready to cross into the Promised Land. Moses tells the people that he is now 120 years old and that God has told him that he will not be leading the people any longer and that Joshua will be the one who leads them to cross the Jordan and take possession of the land that God has promised. Moses also reassures the people (if you don't know the story, they have sent spies to scope out the cities and their inhabitants, and the news wasn't encouraging—see Numbers 13 for the full story) and tells them that the Lord has promised to deal with the inhabitants and destroy them if the people will do exactly as God instructs them. Then in verse 6, Moses tells the people, *"Be strong and courageous; don't be terrified or afraid of them. For it is the Lord your God who goes with you; He will not leave you or forsake you."* As a people who really hadn't done a lot of fighting, this was an encouraging thing to hear.

But then Moses addresses Joshua personally in front of the entire nation and tells him to personally be strong and courageous as he leads them into Canaan (verse 7). He then repeats the promise of God being with him and that He won't leave or forsake him. But now Moses adds that additional fact that not only is God going with him (Joshua), He is also going ahead of him. God promises Joshua in a very personal way that He will already be there when Joshua and the people he is leading arrive. The only thing that God asks is that they do *"exactly as I have commanded you"* (verse 5). So it seems to be very apparent that God's promise to be with His people wherever they are and whatever situation they find themselves in is both a corporate and an individual/personal promise. Of course, this is in keeping with one of God's attributes in that He is omnipresent. He is everywhere at the same time.

I have to admit that during my career in law enforcement, the times that I experienced the most intense fear was on those days or calls that I forgot that God was already there and had promised to never leave or forsake me. Conversely, the times that I was the most fearless was those days when I remembered that God was already there and knew the plans that He had for me. The plans that He had that *"were for my welfare, not for disaster, to give me a future and a hope"* (Jeremiah 29:11). Of course, it wasn't just at work that situations could seem really scary.

For a number of years now, as I previously mentioned, I have supported Northrise University[27] in Ndola, Zambia, and have gone every couple of years to do various work projects. I have taken a

---

[27.] See NorthriseUniversity.com for more information on how God is working there.

number of my children on these excursions as well, both so that they could experience a different culture and learn to work in the service of others. I wanted them to learn and experience the physical demonstration of loving your neighbors. On one of those trips, I had my son and my third daughter who were both young teens. All my travels to and from Zambia had always gone without a hitch, and the trip there was no exception. The trip home, though, did not go according to plan. The route home was to fly to Johannesburg (which has a very nice and modern airport) and then to board that transcontinental flight back to the US. That flight included a stop in Dakar, Senegal, for fuel, passengers, and flight attendant exchange before going on to the US. The problem was that the leg to Johannesburg was full, so we would have to fly on another airline to Dakar and then get our luggage and board the flight to be with the rest of our team on the final leg across the Atlantic.

When we got to Dakar, the almost seamless deboarding and customs checks that I was accustomed to in various other major airports around the globe was nowhere to be seen. To describe it as chaos would be to inadequately describe the scene that my wide-eyed children and I were facing. By the time we finally made it through the checkpoint and had our luggage, we were no longer able to board our flight to the States, and I had no way at that time of letting anyone know what our predicament was. Additionally, I found out that this was the last flight of the night and that the next one was not scheduled until the same time the next evening. We also did not have a visa to enter into Senegal and spend the night, and the next day at this airport was not really a good option either. It was at that moment that an enterprising taxi driver was paying attention to our plight and—realizing that if he didn't have a fare by this point, his night was probably over—approached me.

He told me that he knew of a hotel that Americans and Europeans stay at on the beach and that he could take us there. Being out of options, I agreed, but then things got even more interesting. He escorted us to taxi row (arguing and yelling at a number of his countrymen) and loaded us up, but then his car would not start. So now he had to implore these same men to give him a push start with the three of us loaded up and ready to go. Amazingly enough, they did, and off we went. Our journey, though, took us down dark streets through hard-to-see neighborhoods where the only sign that life existed was the occasional red glow of someone taking a drag off a cigarette in a dark corner of a building. For a brief moment, I began to wonder just what kind of danger that I had put myself and my children into, but it was at that moment that God brought this particular promise back to my mind. I knew that our missing our connection didn't take God by surprise. He didn't have to rework any of His plans for us in that moment. He was already there when we landed and got held up by Senegal security forces. I then realized, for the first time that night, that whatever happened God was in charge and His plan was right on track.

So as not to leave you hanging on the story, the hotel, while it was on the beach, is not to be confused with any sort of four-star resort, but it did meet our needs. There was a restaurant and a room with two beds, so we were able to get some rest and stay in a reasonably secure environment until my new taxi driving friend picked us up the next evening. So now we are back at the airport, our luggage has been checked in, and we have passed through the metal detectors and are in line to board the plane, and I am becoming more relaxed when two Senegalese policemen came up to the line and called out our names and had us step out of line. We were told that we had entered the country illegally (without visas to do so). I explained what had occurred, but their lack of empathy was palpable. I was told that the matter could be settled by the paying of a fine of two hundred dollars apiece, which brought me to my next problem. I didn't have anywhere near that kind of cash on me, and this airport did not have any ATMs (not that I could have withdrawn that much anyway). Now we were about to be taken into custody (oh, I had already shown them my police credentials, but that had failed to impress them as well) when an airline representative offered to let me use their credit card terminal to make the payment to the airline, then she would in turn give the cash to the police officers. After a few moments of discussion among themselves, this seemed to work. A quick swipe of my card and we were told that we could now board the plane (which had finished boarding and was waiting for us while we were dealing with that issue).

Even though I was feeling somewhat anxious at times during this little adventure, God had already gone before me. He had a taxi, a hotel, and a helpful airline employee all in place to show me that He was in control. I have been to Zambia several times since this incident and have continued to take new people with me and have never had problems like this again. But when I do travel, I remember God's plan for me included having me spend the night in Dakar, Senegal, so that I could know in a personal way that when God says for me to not be afraid or discouraged because He is going before me, He means just that. One final note, the airline said that I should not have had to pay for my night in the country and refunded me the six-hundred-dollar ransom that I paid to be able to leave! My God is an awesome God.

MAY

No! We did it for fear that some day your descendants might say to ours, "What do you have to do with the LORD, the God of Israel?" (Joshua 22:24 NIV)

So here is another of the words that the NIV, KJV, and others translate as our word *fear*. The word is *d²âgâh* (pronounced "děh-aw-gaw"), and it comes from a root word that means to be anxious or to take thought of something.[28] Thus, the expanded word here is the idea of anxiety-producing fear. Thus, the rendering of this verse in HCSB is *"We actually did this from a specific concern that in the future your descendants might say to our descendants, 'What relationship do you have with the LORD, the God of Israel?'"*

So now that you have the general idea of this sort of fear, let me put it back into the biblical narrative and tell you what is going on. Joshua and the Israelites have conquered a good portion of the land of Canaan, and portions have been assigned to each of the twelve tribes (except for the priestly tribe of the Levites). The Rubenites, Gadites, and half of the tribe of Mannesseh's land is on the east side of the Jordan River, and so they are feeling cut off from the rest of the nation of Israel, especially as to the ritual religious ceremonies. The leaders of these tribes got it into their heads that at some time in the future, the rest of the tribes might think that they were no longer following after God, so they built a replica altar to show their children and be able to tell them about the proper worship of God. The problem, though, was that the other tribes heard about this altar and

---

[28.] Strong's 1674.

thought that these tribes were trying to start their own worship center apart from where God had directed. They were actually preparing to go to war with the Rubenites and Gadites, but first, they each sent a representative along, with Phinehas the son of Eleazar the priest, to confront them. It was then that they explained what they were doing and that they had no intention of setting up a second location for the ritual sacrifices.

Does this sound familiar? People worry about things that might happen or could happen, and so they start doing things, good and proper things they believe, to alleviate that possible outcome that exists in their imagination. Maybe you've done something like this. You imagined that something could go wrong with a particular situation or relationship, and so you tried to mitigate that outcome before it ever happened. How has that worked out for you or the person that you've seen try? If you or the people are anything like me, your imagination tends to be far more vivid and far more awful than reality turns out to be, so the plans that you develop can be something akin to bringing a sledgehammer to deal with tapping in a finishing nail.

Let's get back to our story first though. Once Phinehas and the ten tribal representatives heard what was really going on, they thought that it was fine and that their cousins on the east side of the Jordan had not rebelled against the directives of God as to where and how He was to be worshipped. Everyone went home happy, and probably relived, and the example altar was actually named Witness, as it showed that Israelites on both sides of the Jordan believed that the Lord is God (Joshua 22:34).[29] To summarize the story, then, one group allowed their imaginations to go places that they didn't need to go, and the other group jumped to conclusions about what the first group was doing, so much so that they were literally ready to go to war over it. At least cooler heads prevailed and a happy ending ensued. Overactive imaginations and jumping to conclusions with-

---

[29]. William MacDonald, *Believer's Bible Commentary* (Nashville, TN: Thomas Nelson Publishers, 1995), 256.

out establishing facts is often the recipe for disaster at all kinds of levels.

Television cop dramas and movies notwithstanding, a great deal of police work has much more to do with keeping the peace than hunting down criminals. Even the live-filmed police shows do not tend to show very much of this side of police work because it isn't exciting or salacious. A mere argument isn't enough to hold either the producers' attention or that of the viewing audience for long, and yet this police function is extremely critical. When people used to ask me what I did, I often joked that I was involved in adult babysitting, as it often felt that way. All too often the temporary resolution was to tell each person to go back to their home and ignore the other person. Parents, does this sound familiar? And yet I would be called out to scene after scene to mediate what was so often a dispute over the most petty of occurrences. But what often exacerbated the situation is that the people involved had imagined that there was intentionality behind the very real action or inaction of the other party's part. Of course, when I questioned them, they had no facts, however remotely construed, to back up why they believed that the other person had intentionally done or not done something that irritated them. Even when I would point that out to them the usual response was something akin to "I just know." Of course, all the logical discourse in the world cannot move someone off a position that they completely believe to be true whether or not there are any articulable facts to support the idea.

Of course, police officers all over the world engage in this kind of peacekeeping behavior because the alternative, like in the story from the book of Joshua, is that people can end up going to actual war. Then crimes are committed. Lives are lost, and property is damaged. Moreover, on the rare occasion that you can bring about a peaceful solution to the real or imagined situation, you leave the call feeling like you have really accomplished something. This is why I always like that part of Jesus's Sermon on the Mount when He said, "*The peacemakers are blessed, for they will be called sons of God*" (Matthew 5:9).

A great lesson from history that shows just how out of hand that imagination can lead to massive disaster is the Sepoy Rebellion of 1857 in India. The East India Company, who was in reality the ruling entity in India at the time, made what at the time was a relatively minor change in the rifles used by their troops. They upgraded to the new Pattern 1853 Enfield rifle, which used greased paper cartridges. In order to open the cartridges and load the rifles, Sepoys had to bite into the paper and tear it with their teeth,[30] and this is where the problem began. Someone's imagination took flight and began spreading rumors in 1856 that the grease on the cartridges was made of a mixture of beef tallow and pork lard.[31] Of course, the eating of cows is forbidden in Hinduism, while consumption of pork is equally forbidden in Islam; and as these were the two major religions in India at the time, virtually their entire local military force was offended that to fire their rifle, they would have to bite into the remains of a forbidden animal. The results of this were that by the time it was over in June of 1858, it is estimated that hundreds of thousands if not a million or more people lost their lives. Instead of establishing what the facts actually were, imagination, speculation, and rumor led to lives lost and a foreign country brought into even greater domination by a foreign power.

Of course, this is fear at its most uncontrollable ugliness, and we are all susceptible to it. Ideas come into our heads, and we fill in the obvious blanks with something that causes us anxiety, and then the next step is to find an immediate-as-possible solution to those factors that are causing us to be afraid. This is where the well-documented fight-or-flight syndrome kicks in. To preserve ourselves we will either run from the supposed danger or take whatever steps are necessary to end the perceived threat. The problem arises, though, when that threat exists primarily in the imagination.

The only way to find true inner peace that allows one to become a peacemaker is to have *"peace with God through our Lord Jesus Christ"*

[30.] Accessed May 31, 2018, https://www.thoughtco.com/the-indian-revolt-of-1857-195476.

[31.] Ibid.

(Romans 5:1). This is the peace that comes only from a right relationship with God, *"the peace of God, which surpasses all understanding"* (Philippians 4:7 CSB). From that position then, when you know (not just feel or hope) that you belong to the king of kings, does the lack of peace that fear produces dissipate like a drop of water on a hot sidewalk in July.

*　　*　　*　　*　　*

> I said to you: I am Yahweh (the Lord) your God. Do not fear the gods of the Amorites whose land you live in. But you did not obey Me. (Judges 6:10)

If you have never read or studied the book of Judges in the Old Testament, it is a long history of the downward spiral of the nation of Israel before they became a kingdom. Of course, they didn't fare much better than either, but that story will wait for a later time. Essentially what you will find is that the people would move away from God. He would allow them to be dominated by an evil foreign presence. The people would then cry out to God for deliverance, and God would send someone to deliver them. Once peace was established, the cycle would start all over again, but like any downward spiral, each judge was a little less than the previous and the people's rebellion to God's law was a bit worse. Today's verse comes from the beginning of the story of Gideon who was the fifth in line in this cycle.

Chapter 6 starts, as does the beginning of every cycle, with a statement that *"the Israelites did what was evil in the sight of the Lord"* (Judges 6:1). The oppressing people this time was the Midianites along with their allies the Amalekites. The land of Midian is in the northwest corner of present-day Saudi Arabia. They were distant relatives of the Israelites, as they came from the later sons of Abraham (Midian was a son of Abraham and his wife Keturah). Apparently, they were nomadic raiders who were very numerous, as the Bible describes them as coming to ravage the Israeli crops like a great swarm of locusts (verse 5) and that they and their camels were without number (verse 5). So the story, then, in a nutshell, is that the nation of Israel was beginning to starve to death because the Midianites would come in, devour their crops and pastureland, then leave them nothing to live on; and this had been going on for seven long years. So the people again cry out to God for deliverance, and here is how He responds through a prophet:

> *This is what the LORD, the God of Israel, says: I brought you up out of Egypt, out of the land of slavery. I rescued you from the hand of the Egyptians. And I delivered you from the hand of all your oppressors; I drove them out before you and gave you their land. I said to you, 'I am the LORD your God; do not worship the gods of the Amorites, in whose land you live.' But you have not listened to me.*

If you know your Bible, this entire statement sounds really familiar and should have to the Israelites as well.

Let's go back to when God essentially created the nation of Israel when He redeemed them, as He reminded them in the above passage, from the oppression of Egypt. They came to Mount Sinai, and God gave them His covenantal law in Exodus 20, the famous ten words or as we know them, the Ten Commandments. This was how God began the giving of His law in the first three verses: "*Then God spoke all these words: I am the Lord your God, who brought you out of the land of Egypt, out of the place of slavery. Do not have other gods besides me.*" Looks kind of familiar, doesn't it? So now we know exactly why the Israelites were under God's judgment. As a people, they had violated the very first commandment. They had given their fear, their reverence, and awe to the false gods of the Amorites whom they lived by.

The area that Israel occupied was surrounded by people groups who held to the worship and belief in many gods. The idea that was rampant in this polytheism was that "no one god was ultimate, and gods were believed to be finite and not absolute. No one god was believed to possess unlimited wisdom or power."[32] God reminded His people that these were false beliefs, and He again cited His own work to bring them out of Egypt and make them into a nation as evidence of this. He also told them, in very clear language, that they had violated the very first commandment that He gave them.

Let's look at that first commandment, which has been called the foundation for the other nine that follow it. This is the principle of *Soli Deo gloria*: "glory to God alone." In this first commandment, God uses the second person singular, and unless you're a language geek, that doesn't really mean anything to you. What it does mean is that by speaking in this way, God indicates that each individual of the nation was addressed personally and was required as an individual to obey the law; a mere general national obedience would be insufficient.[33] With this personal application of the first commandment in mind, let's break it down a bit further. The first phrase "Do not have" means to not have or to keep from having a relationship with. We are, as individuals, to keep from having a relationship with anything before God. This is a very broad statement because we can, and do, effectively put our trust in and show fidelity to a lot of things that don't look like a traditional idol.

The next phrase to examine is "Besides Me." This doesn't mean that it's okay to worship other things as long as we put God first in line. This phrase really means "Before My face." The concept of the word *face* has really entered our culture. Many were the time when I would be talking to someone, generally someone whom I was accusing of a wrongdoing, and they would tell me to "get out of my face" even though I was several feet away. It wasn't as if I was anything close to going nose-to-nose with them, but what I was doing was putting my case of what they had done wrong right before them. Similarly, God tells people to not put something that they effectually worship in His presence. Setting up a false deity is like insulting God to his

---

32. Mark F. Rooker, *The Ten Commandments: Ethics for the Twenty-First Century* (Nashville, TN: B&H Academic, 2010), 24.
33. Phillip Graham Ryken, *Written in Stone: The Ten Commandments and Today's Moral Crisis* (Phillipsburg, NJ: P&R Publishing, 2003), 61.

face.[34] And since one of God's attributes is that He is omnipresent (everywhere at all times), people, especially His people, are not to put anything in God's place at any time or place.

In this section's verse, God called out His people because they had again feared, or given their respect and fidelity to, someone else other than Yahweh. When we go to museums and look at the artifacts of ancient cultures, one of the things that is almost always on display is the representations that various cultures made of their gods. For the most part, particularly in our Western culture, you really don't see that sort of thing. But really, a false god can be anything, even a good thing, which we focus on to the exclusion of the one true God.[35] Things like our job, our spouse, our children, or even the practice of a religion. But the number 1 false god that I and many people I know regularly return to is the god known as the self. Of course, self seems to be the god of this age. Our advertisements ("You deserve…"), our public education (the altar of self-esteem), and everything else around us point us to venerate ourselves as the center of our own universe. Oscar Wilde wrote that to love oneself is the beginning of a life-long romance,[36] and Christians fall into this violation of the first commandment almost as much as the rest of society around us. A quick survey of how Christians spend their time and you will find that a lot of us spend far too much time thinking about what we need, what we want, and how we are going to achieve getting what we want and the problems that are in the way of achieving them.

All this self-centered thinking has led us right back to a form of pluralism that promotes the "many paths to God" concept. We want our religion to be right for us and to conform to our wants, needs, and desires as opposed to allegiance to God and what He wants. The problem here, though, is that we are highly imperfect creatures, and so any concept or way of doing something will carry that imperfec-

---

[34.] Godfrey William Ashby, *Go Out and Meet God: A Commentary on the Book of Exodus* (Grand Rapids, MI: International Theological Commentary, 1998), 88.

[35.] Phillip Graham Ryken, *Written in Stone: The Ten Commandments and Today's Moral Crisis* (Phillipsburg, NJ: P&R Publishing, 2003), 66.

[36.] Oscar Wilde, quoted in Michael S. Horton's *The Law of Perfect Freedom* (Chicago: Moody, 1993), 56.

tion with it. God, on the other hand, is perfect, so His prescribed way of coming into His presence is perfect; and because it is perfect, it doesn't change through time or circumstance or culture. It cannot, or otherwise it wouldn't be perfect. Because God is perfect, there cannot be multiple paths to His presence. There can only be the perfect way, God's way, which is by grace through faith in the perfect work of Jesus Christ. Anything else is to join those ancient Israelites in fearing a false god or gods.

*   *   *   *   *

> And Jotham ran away, and fled, and went to Beer, and dwelt there, for fear of Abimelech his brother. (Judges 9:21 ASV)

In this verse, we come to yet another of the Hebrew words that has been translated in the King James and other versions into the word *fear*. It is the word *pânâym* (pronounced "paw-neem") that comes from the root word *pânâh*, which means to turn or to look. So this word, then, has the idea of turning the face away from something that is worrisome or frightening. Think of being in a horror movie and looking away when the monster or the killer is beginning to attack the victim of the moment. Because I am now officially old, for me that was the movie *Jaws*. Of course, it was enhanced by the two-note music score that announced when the shark was preparing to attack the next victim. More than one person in the theatre watched those shark attack scenes through their fingers or by the furtive glance until the attack was through.

Let me put this verse back into the context of the biblical story from which it came. We need answers to the questions of just who is Jotham and Abimelech and why is Jotham running away, literally turning his face in fear, from Abimelech? This story happens at the end of Gideon's life, and it is noted in Judges 8:28 that after the defeat of the Midianites, the land was peaceful for forty years. We also learn that Gideon (meaning "warrior"),[37] who was also known as Jerubbaal (meaning "Baal will contend")[38] after he destroyed the altar to Baal, had an incredible seventy sons by a number of wives and a son by a concubine, who was named Abimelech. As soon as Gideon died, the Israelites went back to worshipping Baal (there's that first-commandment violation again) and forgot *the Lord their God who had delivered them from the power of the enemies around them*" (Judges 8:34). Now the family drama begins, as Abimelech goes for a power grab. He starts by going to his mother's (the concubine, not a wife) brothers and fostered dissension as he asked them if they wanted to be ruled by the seventy sons of Jerubbaal (notice that he uses this name, which reminds them that his father was the one who had destroyed the altar to Baal) or whether it would be better to be ruled by just one man who was their blood relative. They found this to be amenable and gave him money from the temple to Baal-berith (Baal of the covenant),[39] which he used to hire a bunch of thugs. With that group in place, he went to Gideon's home in Ophrah and killed all but one of his brothers, Jotham, the youngest who hid on a large stone. With the family of Gideon wiped out, Abimelech was made king by the Lords of Shechem.

Jotham, though, apparently had some of his father's warrior spirit, as he went up to the top of Mount Gerizim and yelled down to Abimelech a long parable (Judges 9:7–15) that predicted the destruction of both Abimelech and the people who had put him into power, which came to pass about three years later when Abimelech, who was again trying to kill a bunch of people, had a woman push the upper portion of a millstone off the roof and it fractured Abimelech's skull. He lived just long enough to request that his armor-bearer kill him so that his reputation wouldn't be sullied by having been killed by a woman. This section's verse comes at the end of Jotham's prediction that Abimelech and the lords of Shechem would destroy one another. So can you see the scene in your mind? There's Jotham all

---

[37.] Strong's 1439.
[38.] Strong's 3378.
[39.] Strong's 1170.

alone, standing at the top of a mountain and yelling at Abimelech, his thugs, and the leading men of Shechem. Then when he's done, he runs off because he is justifiably afraid of his brother who has already killed all the rest of their brothers.

Have you ever experienced something like this? And no, I don't mean having one of your siblings murder the rest of your siblings. I'm referring to Jotham, standing at a safe distance and yelling at someone before running off. Now I'm not condemning Jotham at all. He was a marked man and at a great disadvantage. What he did was actually remarkably brave in the light of everything that had just happened. He prophesized what was going to happen to all those evil men, but then instead of trusting the Lord who had given him that prophecy, he saw the strength of those that opposed him; and then fear overtook him, and he turned and ran.

Family battles can be devastating, ugly, and even extremely violent. Often there is that one person in the family who uses either physical or verbal violence to dominate everyone else. Fear is their method of controlling various situations for their own real or perceived benefit. While I am fortunate enough to not have experienced this in my own family, I have seen it over and over again in other family environments. It usually takes a Jotham to stand up in opposition before it ends, and as often as not in my experience, the situation usually gets worse for a time before it gets better. It just takes one person to put aside their fear and stand up to the wrong that is being fostered upon the rest of the family, something that is much easier said than done.

> Samuel lay down until the morning; then
> he opened the doors of the Lord's house. He was
> afraid to tell Eli the vision. (1 Samuel 3:15)

To this point, we have only dealt with adults, but now this story brings us to the concept of fear and children. In Gill's Exposition of the Bible, he notes that Samuel was "according to Josephus (n), and others, now about twelve years of age."[40] He was living with the high priest Eli at Shiloh because his mother, Hannah, had been barren, and she asked God to give her a son that she in turn would then dedicate to be in full service to God. God answered her prayer, and so after she had weaned her son, she took him to be raised into full-time service in the place of worship with the high priest Eli. So at this point in the story, Samuel has been living and working around the tabernacle for several years and has now reached the age that many of associate with children in about the sixth grade. Generally, the priest-hood was handed down from father to son, and Eli had two sons by the names of Hophni and Phinehas who had been raised in service at the tabernacle but they, as the Bible puts it, *were wicked men; they had not regard for the Lord or for the priests share of the sacrifices from the people*" (1 Samuel 2:12). Essentially, they got greedy and wanted more and better portions of the animal sacrifices for themselves than the Mosaic Law stipulated, and they used bullying tactics to get what they wanted. They were in fact stealing from the Lord. Oh and one more thing, they were sleeping with the women who served at the entrance to the tent of meetings. But not only were they guilty but Eli was as well because he knew about it and allowed it to continue to happen.

Toward the end of chapter 2 of 1 Samuel, it states that a man of God came to Eli and gave him the Word of God that he and his house were under judgment for the evil that had occurred and that in fact his two sons were going to die on the same day. Samuel's devotion to the Lord, though, was in stark contrast to Hophni and Phinehas, as he would actually sleep in the tabernacle presumably so that he could faithfully attend to his duties. So now you have the picture, a twelve-year-old boy who is faithful to the service of God living with a household that has become completely corrupt and self-serving in their role as the religious leaders of Israel. Then one night God calls Samuel, apparently audibly. As he hears it, he thinks that it is Eli calling him. He goes in and asks what Eli wants, only to be told

40. Gill's Exposition of the Bible, accessed through BibleHub.com, accessed June 1, 2018, http://biblehub.com/commentaries/gill/1_samuel/3.htm.

that Eli hadn't called him, and so he went and laid back down. The same scene repeats twice more until finally Eli figures out that it must be God speaking to him, and so he gives young Samuel wise council and tells him that if it happens again, he should respond with "*Speak, Lord, for your servant is listening.*" So this time when he lays down, Samuel is ready.

God reaffirms to this boy what the man of God had earlier said to Eli in some very strong language ending with the statement that "*the iniquity of Eli's family will never be wiped out by either sacrifice or offering*" (1 Samuel 3:14). Then when God finishes what He had to say, Samuel went back to sleep until morning. The fact that Samuel could go back to sleep after just hearing God speak to him, to me, is amazing. I personally would have been on an adrenaline rush that would probably have lasted for hours! The next morning, Samuel gets up and begins his day, but as this section's verse points out, he was afraid to tell Eli what he had heard. This is understandable given his circumstances and what the atmosphere was like that Hophni and Phineas had brought to be while Eli chose to ignore it. It almost seems unfair to some people that God had given such a task to a boy as young as Samuel. What other normal reaction could he have but to be afraid? And yet as always, God knew what He was doing, and when Eli asked him to repeat what God had said, Samuel *told him everything and did not hide anything from him* (1 Samuel 3:18). Wow! We see honesty, bravery, and integrity on display.

It's amazing how young children are when they learn to lie. The internet is replete with videos of young children boldly lying about not eating something while the evidence against them is quite literally smeared across their faces. While these videos are somewhat humorous, it still reminds me that we are all born with a sin nature. It is natural for us to lie or to obfuscate the truth to the point where the truth is no longer recognizable. But Samuel repeats God's Word and doesn't leave anything out even though it had to make him really uncomfortable. Now I know many of you have faced something like this. How did you fare when the pressure was on and telling the whole truth was about to make you or someone else really uncomfortable? Many are the times that I folded and tried to mitigate the results, only to have it blow up even worse later on. Proverbs 27:6 says, "*The wounds of a friend are trustworthy, but the kisses of an enemy are excessive.*" While telling the truth may be difficult or uncomfortable at times, if we do it with the right mindset, from love for the person we are talking to (Ephesians 4:15), then the fear that we initially feel will dissipate to be replaced by the same honesty and integrity that was on display in the life of Samuel. Fear comes when we love ourselves over others.

JUNE

> Saul answered Samuel, "I have sinned. I
> have transgressed the Lord's command and your
> words. Because I was afraid of the people, I
> obeyed them." (1 Samuel 15:24)

So let me put this fear response back into its context. Saul is the king
of the Israelites, and as with most kings, whatever he says goes. Back
at the beginning of this chapter, Samuel (the prophet of God at that
time—essentially God's spokesperson) brings him a directive of God.
Back when the people were involved in the exodus from Egypt, the
Amalekites had continually attacked and harassed the Israelites (see
Exodus 17:8), and now God directed Saul to go and wipe them and
their possessions out of existence. The wording in verse 3 is very
specific on this point, as it reads, *"Now go and attack the Amalekites
and completely destroy everything they have. Do not spare them. Kill men
and women, children and infants, oxen and sheep, camels and donkeys."*

You may be wondering just who these people were and why the
animosity. The Amalekites were a cousin people group to the Israelites
as they were descendants of one of Esau's (Jacob's older twin brother)
grandsons named Amalek. According to *Ellicott's Commentary for
English Readers*, this hostility may have not been unwarranted. They
were probably the main people group in the area of what we would
now see as the southern part of Israel and the northern portion of
the Sinai Peninsula. Their hostility probably came from the perceived need to defend their summer and autumn pastureland. It is
believed that they probably saw the Israelites as "intruders, robbers,

persons entitled to scant favor at their hands."[41] It is most likely that it was the way that they went about it that really got them in trouble. Deuteronomy 25:17–18 describes their methodology: *"Remember what the Amalekites did to you on the journey after you left Egypt. They met you along the way and attacked all your stragglers from behind when you were tired and weary. They did not fear God."* So because as a people they did not fear God (always the primary offense) and just attacked and killed the feeble and weary at the rear of the march, God's judgment is that they and all their possessions are to be completely destroyed. The problem arises, as it always does, when people decide to only kinda and sorta follow God's commands. Remember, no person or animal was to be left alive.

Let's go back now to 1 Samuel 15 and pick up the story in verse 8 after Saul and the Israelite army defeats the Amalekites: *"He captured Agag king of Amalek alive, but he* [Saul edition note] *completely destroyed all the rest of the people with the sword. Saul and the troops spared Agag, and the best of the sheep, cattle, and fatlings, as well as the young rams and the best of everything else. They were not willing to destroy them, but they did destroy all the worthless and unwanted things."* So instead of obeying God's directive, Saul and his army decided that they could benefit financially by keeping all the really good animals for themselves. Of course, God saw it all and sent Samuel to confront Saul about the disobedience and, like a young child, caught their hands in the cookie jar. Saul's first response was to lie as he pleaded his case. He told Samuel that he had obeyed God's directive in attacking the Amalekites and that the reason that they now had all these prized animals was so that they could offer a sacrifice to God. I really like Samuel's response in verses 22–23: *"Then Samuel said: Does the LORD take pleasure in burnt offerings and sacrifices as much as in obeying the LORD? Look: <u>to obey is better than sacrifice; to pay attention is better than the fat of rams</u>* [underline added]. *For rebellion is like the sin of divination, and defiance is like wickedness and idolatry. Because you have rejected the word of the LORD, He has rejected you as king."* Now

---

[41.] Ellicott's Commentary for English Readers on BibleHub.com., accessed on July 5, 2018, biblehub.com/commentaries/Ellicott /exodus/17.htm.

you see this section's verse on fear. Saul was still not taking ownership of his sin and instead gave another reason for his disobedience. He was afraid of the people whom he was king over and just sort of went along with the decision to not follow God's command.

My guess is that all of us can relate to this. Even if you can't (or don't choose to) remember a time when you only sort of did what you were told, if you are a parent, I know that you have seen this in one or more of your children. We have all been at that point where we thought that what we were told to do was stupid and that we knew something better. A lot of times, like Saul and the Israelite army, we try to justify it with something positive for the person who gave the order in the first place: "I know I didn't do it the way that you told me to, but I did it this way for you." In my police world, as a paramilitary organization, when an order is given by your superior, it is expected that you will carry it out without deviation. If you see a major flaw, you can bring it to their attention, but if they do not change their directive, then you are to carry it out (unless of course, if it is blatantly illegal). The advantage to that is if something untoward occurs, the onus is on the one who gave the order in the first place. If you deviate from what you were told and things go sideways, then you will bear the brunt of responsibility for whatever went wrong. That is exactly where Saul found himself, having to bear the responsibility for what he and the army he led had failed to do, and he blamed his greed and disobedience on fear.

Taking what Saul said at face value, that he disobeyed because he was afraid that his army would turn on him, is that ever an acceptable excuse for disobedience? This kind of fear is really a lack of trust in the one who is giving the command. What Saul and his army were really saying by disobeying God was that they did not trust Him to meet their needs, and now they saw a way to meet their needs without God. This is really reminiscent of the adage "God helps those who help themselves." Then they want to justify the disobedience by putting a religious spin on it. Disobeying God's commands in the name of serving Him is just a thinly veiled way to disobey and do what you wanted to do all along, which is serving yourself. Disobedience always puts you in charge. It makes you the god of your life, which of course is a direct violation of the first of the Ten Commandments: "You shall have no other gods before me" (Exodus 20:3).

Some level of fear when we disobey is actually a healthy thing if we react to it properly. If we respond by either stopping the disobedient act to begin with or later by acknowledging that we disobeyed, enter into true remorse for our actions without attempting to justify them, and seek forgiveness while endeavoring to learn so as to not repeat the error, then that initial fear response can be a good thing. On the other hand, if we react to the fear in a way that merely seeks to mitigate or diffuse the consequences, then we are still trying to do what we want to do and just not have to pay the consequences either in full or in part. We are still trying to be our own god. This response to fear leaves us in the same state that we entered the disobedience in to begin with. Like Saul, when we get caught doing something wrong or are confronted with it after the act is done, we are initially afraid because of the possible consequences. And the reaction to that is rarely remorse, or if we do express some level of remorse, it is often what my wife calls junior-high-girl sorry. You know what that is? It is the half-hearted (at best) "I'm sorry" with no true feeling of sorrow or remorse. It is usually accompanied with either an eye roll or an emotionless stare off into the distance and is satisfying to no one.

When you feel that kind of fear coming on, what do you do? Panic, lie, redirect the blame, and/or try to find a positive justification. It is difficult and not the natural thing to do, but try to just confess. Admit that you did (or perhaps intentionally did not do what you were supposed to do) it and you will find that your internal stress diminishes almost instantly. In my career, I observed this over and over again. I would be interviewing a suspect that I knew had committed the crime. They were trying all the wrongs (but natural responses) and were tense and often in a visible state of panic. The moment that they gave up and admitted to the crime, I could see a visible change in their body. They would become more relaxed and much less adversarial. Now that is not to say that they did not sometimes go back to some of those other responses during the booking process, but in a lot of cases, now they could just be themselves, and the entire process was much easier for both of us.

*   *   *   *   *

When the disciples saw Him walking on the
sea, they were terrified. "It's a ghost!" they said,
and cried out in fear. (Matthew 14:26)

My wife and I like going to the movies. Movies, softball, and church group activities made up most of our dates before we got married, and going to the movies has continued to be one of our favorite escapes when we can find the time to go. Neither of us, though, has ever been a fan of the horror genre or tales involving hauntings and the like. It's not the fact that we don't believe in the existence of ghosts (we don't), it's just that we do not particularly like having things jump out at us or people trying to overcome supernatural evil through their own power. But this idea of some otherworldly apparitions being involved in our world has been around throughout recorded time, as people have attempted to explain that unexplained bump in the night or that shadowy movement that is always just at the corner of our vision or off in the distance that we can't easily explain. And as we have already discussed, the unknown is always a basis for fear because we do not know how to handle it.

In this verse on fear, we have the disciples in a boat out on the Sea of Galilee (actually a large freshwater lake). This body of water is approximately 33 miles in circumference, about 13 miles long, and 8.1 miles wide at the widest point. At the direction of Jesus, the disciples are to cross to a city on the other side of the lake while he goes off to pray. Now several of the disciples were former professional fisherman on this very body of water, so they knew all the tricks of the trade for surviving on the water. The event that they had just been a witness to earlier that day was when Jesus had been preaching to a crowd of thousands and had just fed them all from a boy's lunch of five loaves and two fish. They had actually watched as Jesus created and prepared food and over and over again until everyone was fed and the disciples had collected twelve baskets full of leftovers! So now you have the general context for what happens next.

While the story is pretty dramatic in and of itself, Dr. Michael S. Heiser, in his book *I Dare You Not to Bore Me with the Bible,* observes that the cultural context for Jesus revealing Himself was far more significant than just the fact that He was walking on the water in the midst of a storm. Dr. Heiser points out that an unpredictable and deadly sea was a well-known symbol of nature in a state of disorder. This disorder was also pictured as a sea monster called Leviathan or Rahab, and other cultures had their own sea monsters that would make the sea an unpredictable and unsafe place, especially for people who were far more accustomed to life on land. Dr. Heister writes that "religions across the ancient Mediterranean often depicted their important deities destroying or subduing the sea dragon, thereby calming the sea, and restoring order,"[42] thereby making it safe for people to sail. Of course, the Bible says that it is Yahweh who has put order in the universe. In Job 26, we see the picture of God restoring order by the killing of the sea monster known as Rahab. Verses 12–13 reads, "*By His power He stirred the sea, and by His understanding He crushed Rahab. By His breath the heavens gained their beauty; His hand pierced the fleeing serpent.*" One of David's singers composed Psalm 89, and he also talks about God's sovereignty over the sea by the destruction of the sea monster Rahab in verses 9–10: "*You rule the raging sea; when its waves surge, you still them. You crushed Rahab like one who is slain; you scattered your enemies with your powerful arm.*"

The imagery continues through the end of time and God's ultimate victory. Isaiah 27:1 says, "*On that day the LORD with His harsh, great, and strong sword, will bring judgment on Leviathan, the fleeing serpent—Leviathan, the twisting serpent. He will slay the monster that is in the sea.*" Daniel's prophecy of the end times has the image of four nonaquatic beasts that emerge from a stormy sea (Daniel 7:1–8). They come from chaos that is a storm and the sea, which is a repre-

---

42. Michael S. Heiser, *I Dare You Not to Bore Me with the Bible,* accessed July 4, 2018, excerpt located at www.biblestudymagazine.com/bible-study-magazine-blog/2018/4/17/what-walking-on-water-really-means.

sentation of evil. Then when the final battle with evil is over, God says that He will make a new heaven and a new earth, but you will notice that according to Revelation 21:1, *the sea no longer existed.* There is no longer a place where the order of God's creation can be disturbed.

Now let's get back to the New Testament where we see Jesus as the Lord over the sea. John and the others knew the writings of the Old Testament, and now they see that Jesus is the one who subdues the forces of chaos and imposed His will on the waters and everything the waters represent.[43] But grasping that was initially difficult, so their first reaction was that it was a ghost because they knew that no mere man could walk on water. Like a scene in a modern horror movie, this event jumped out at the disciples, and it took a minute to realize who it was and what was happening. Do you see the complete context now? The disciples had been a part of an incredible miracle where Jesus had met the needs of thousands of people. Next came the pop quiz. Jesus sent them out on the lake, into an area of their strength and experience and right into the teeth of a storm that He knew was coming. Would they still trust Him even in the middle of this seemingly uncontrolled chaos? The story concludes with John recognizing Jesus and taking a least a few steps in faith as he, too, walks on the water. Of course, he loses focus and starts to sink, and Jesus rescues him and instantly calms the storm. So the fear in this story is really a combination of the fear that comes from the feeling that you are not in control of your situation combined with a bit of the fear of the unexplainable like a man walking on the water.

* * * * *

As a pretty classic type A personality (as a majority of police officers are), I hate the feeling of being in a situation that I'm not in control of. A great deal of my training was in how to control a situation by various means, including voice techniques, physical positioning, and trying to make sure that we outnumber the bad guys.

[43.] Ibid.

After almost three decades of doing that, I've learned to be in control of most situations or to at least seem like I am, which allows me to put forth a relatively calm demeanor most of the time. That feeling of being in control of a situation also helps to really allay any fear, but of course, all too often it was merely just a well-crafted facade designed to lessen my own fear and that of those that I was trying to help. On one particular incident early on in my career, we had just transitioned to a new portable radio that stayed on your belt with a cord that went to a shoulder mike. It is pretty much standard now, but back in the early 1990s, that was new cutting-edge stuff. One of the concerns that a lot of the senior officers expressed was that the cord could be used to strangle you with, but of course, all of us new young guns thought that was ridiculous until it happened to me.

I was about to arrest a landlord who was really mistreating his renters (illegals who felt that they couldn't call the police for fear of being deported). He and I really didn't like each other and had gotten into a rather heated verbal exchange, and I kept egging him on in the hope that he would do something foolish like take a swing at me (you see, he didn't like not being in control either!), which he obliged me by doing so. As he did, I stepped back so that I could use all the defensive tactics that I had been taught, but then the chaos moment happened. The small child of the couple that was being abused ran behind me, and I tripped over him and fell to the ground with the outraged landlord right on top of me. I landed on my belly with the landlord on top of me, and the next thing that I knew, he had my radio cord around my neck, and the pressure was on. Moreover, he outweighed me by at least thirty pounds, so I was trapped. I instinctively grabbed at that cord with both hands, which allowed me to maintain my airway; but your hands were also your most effective offensive weapon, and they were now out of commission making sure that I could breathe, and I was suddenly very afraid. I had a partner there, and she was doing everything that she could, but she was smaller than I was and deadly force was not an option because the landlord and I were tangled up together. She finally (before I go much further, this entire event happened in seconds; you probably have taken more time to read about it than the actual event) applied a strike to his head with her flashlight, and this stunned him just enough that he released his death grip on the cord around my neck. Now I could reengage, and soon he was in custody with a nice knot on his head and a broken hand to show for his effort.

But we all get those moments when chaos seems to be in control. Everything around us looks like a disaster, and we don't see any way of either controlling it or surviving it. Like the disciples, all our experience and expertise suddenly seem worthless. But that is the exact moment that we find out if our trust is in someone trustworthy. I had faith that my partner was doing everything that she could to make sure that I didn't die that day. But more importantly, I believed then, and still do today, that only God is the controller of both life and death and that my faith in Him to bring me through the situation was incontrovertible.

*   *   *   *   *

There is no fear in love; instead, perfect love drives out fear, because fear involves punishment. So the one who fears has not reached perfection in love. (1 John 4:18)

The idea of love implies some level of attraction, whether it is physical, mental, emotional, or some combination of those elements. Fear, on the other hand, usually has a component of revulsion. At the beginning of this book, I told you that I have a fairly definite fear of spiders. And that fear hasn't been helped by seeing close-up pictures of arachnids. My guess is that at some time or another, most of you have seen those pictures, and for me, there is nothing beautiful about them. The revulsion wells up in me, and I reconfirm with myself that I don't like spiders and I move on. I wasn't always afraid of spiders. As a young boy, I would find one, let it crawl on my finger or hand, and then gently shake it off so that it would save itself by spinning a web attached to my hand. Playing with small spiders was no big deal until my family moved to Palmdale, California. While California is a lovely state and I love to visit there, there are some places that I believe should not be inhabited my man, and the area around Palmdale is one of them. Now I am sure that there are people that say the same thing about Phoenix, especially in the summer, so we will just chalk it up to my opinion then.

In the brief year that I lived in Palmdale, there was an infestation of black widow spiders. They were everywhere. They are a particularly aggressive and venomous spider whose web is not the beautiful and symmetrical design that so many spiders produce. A black widow's web looks more like something made by a creature with severe OCD on acid. There are very sticky strings of web going every which way over a given area. And those nasty little creatures had invaded our garage, turning it into something out of a horror movie. My brothers and I were instructed to never go in there. This was one of our parent's instructions that we obeyed without argument. Then one morning, I woke up instantly. It was one of those times when you go from dead asleep to wide awake because one of your senses has told your brain that you need to be fully conscious right now. I usually slept shirtless with just pajama bottoms, and when I woke up, I was lying on my back with the sheets down somewhere around my waist and I was aware of something moving across my chest. Without moving anything other than my eyes, I looked down to see a large, shiny female black widow crawling across me. Talk about fear and revulsion! Since the spider didn't seem like it was interested in biting me and was moving right along, I elected to lay still not even breathing until she completed traversing me and headed down the side of my bed. With my heart pounding out of my chest, I jumped out of the other side of my bed, grabbed one of my slippers, and turned that spider into a large moist spot on the wall where she now was. And thus began my fear and repulsion with all arachnid kind.

I can tell you that I did not love that spider crawling across me. There was no trust, which left only fear. The verse for this section says that perfect love drives our fear. There are really two main words here that allow us to understand the verse: *love* and *perfect*. The word *perfect* means to be complete. In the realm of human relationship, then, the concept of maturity will also be involved. So the type of love that drives out fear is one that is mature and complete. So by extrapolation then, it is something that we have to grow into, much like we have to grow to mature physically. A mature or complete love is one that looks and acts like the love of the Father, a love that is so complete that He gave up His own son so that we could be redeemed back to a place where we can begin to appropriate that kind of love into our own lives. This kind of love is also extremely confident. It is focused not on self but on the God who created the universe by simply speaking it into existence. There is no doubt in that kind of love when it is complete and mature.

Fear, on the other hand, from what I read, either remembers an incident in the past and projects it forward (what a lot of us refer to as a phobia); looks at something in the present that is not understood or controlled, leading to an uncertain outcome; or looks at the future and sees a possible threat that must be removed. But a person who has a perfect love that is focused on God does not have any reason to fear the past, present, or future. Here are a couple of verses to bolster your boldness to help you grow into that kind of perfect love with which fear cannot abide. God has promised that eventually *we shall be like Him* (Jesus) when He returns (1 John 3:1–2). While just having the hope that I'll get there someday is great, there is an even better promise in the next chapter. 1 John 4:17 says, "*In this, love is perfected with us so that we may have confidence in the day of judgment, for we are as He is in this world.*" Really focus in on that last phrase "for we are as He is in this world." Positionally, we are already there! We are like Christ in this world.

Now I've been a Christian for a long time, and there are a lot of times that I do not act or sound like Jesus. I'm still in the process of being conformed to that image, but what I do have is the ability and the authority to tap into the perfect love that Jesus displayed because I have the Holy Spirit living within me. I have to just step out of the way and let Him control me. Of course, it is so easy to say the word *just* like it is as simple as throwing a light switch when you walk into a room. To step out of the way means that I have to completely subjugate my will. To say as Jesus did, "*Not my will but yours*" (Luke 22:42). While it is a bit easier now to do this, it is still a very real struggle on a daily basis, and when I grab on to my own will, fear is only a step behind.

Finally, did you see what fear is focused on? The answer is punishment, which means pain in either the physical, emotional, or spiritual plane. When that spider was walking across me, I was afraid of some really intense physical pain. I have never actually been bitten, but I have heard from people who have, and I am confident that it is something that I don't want to experience. Likewise, perfect love has no fear because of the knowledge that "*therefore, no condemnation now exists for those in Christ Jesus*" (Romans 8:1). I no longer stand condemned before God for anything that I have done or will do because Jesus has already paid the penalty and I have accepted that free gift. But I still have to grow into that likeness until the day that God completes it and I am fully like Christ.

What a lot of people do, even many Christians, is try to go back and to be punished for something that they've already been forgiven for. This doesn't make sense, but it is a very real thing. Punishment or the prospect thereof brings fear; so then like the verse says, if I'm afraid, then I don't have a complete or perfect love, and instead the possibility of punishment and the pain it brings becomes what I focus on. This results in fear. As a born-again Christian, I have no fear of any future judgment because I know that everything I've done or will do that is in opposition to God and His perfection has had the punishment already meted out. So no punishment means no pain. No pain means no fear. John 5:24 says, "*I assure you: Anyone who hears My word and believes Him who sent Me has eternal life and will not come under judgment but has passed from death to life.*" I do not have to try to be good enough or make sure that I correctly follow a set of religious edicts. I only have to believe that Jesus lived, died, and rose again. Of course, that belief means that I accept that Jesus is the Lord of life and death and therefore God. Then according to Romans 10:9, the only thing that I have to do on the physical plane is confess with my mouth that I believe. So simply put, tell others. Nothing else is required!

Well, we have covered a lot of fear so far in these first six chapters, and we haven't even begun to fully examine every verse that mentions the word *fear* or *afraid*. As you are beginning to see, fear in one form or another has dominated my life, but I am thankful to say that the control and the severity of fear in my life is much less than it was. God has been faithful to bring me along in my life's journey and work on perfecting my love for him. It's taken a long time, and not because God isn't powerful but because I am stubborn and I believe Him that eventually He will bring me to the place where my love is perfected and fear no longer exists. But let's move forward and grab some more aspects of fear and see what God has to say about it.

JULY

To fear the LORD is to hate evil. I hate
arrogant pride, evil conduct, and perverse speech.
(Proverbs 8:13)

The wise fear the LORD and shun evil, but
a fool is hotheaded and yet feels secure. (Proverbs
14:16 NIV)

The fear mentioned in these two verses is that reverential awe and respect that should be in place when we think about God. In the book of Proverbs, wisdom (the correct application of knowledge) is pictured as a woman who is trying to teach a young man her ways. In Proverbs 1:7, it says that *the fear of the LORD is the beginning of knowledge*," but then in chapter 8, we get a definition of what that fear looks like in practical terms, and that starts with hating or shunning evil. But that is still a bit too general, so God makes it more specific and says that He hates arrogant pride, evil conduct, and perverse speech, which indicates that we should as well when they show up in our lives. The problem with hating evil is that it is so pervasive. Really, what hasn't been affected by evil in some way or another? Am I then to hate everything around me? That doesn't make much sense, so let's examine the three things (not an exhaustive list by any means) that God says He hates arrogant pride, evil conduct, and perverse speech.

If I am going to think about God correctly (fear Him), then the first order of business is to bring up my arrogant pride. Pride is the root sin from which all other sin grows, and it shows up early in our development. When my oldest daughter was just a toddler and learning to put sentences together, she already showed the strength and independence that is all too common in first-born children. This showed up in a phrase that our family still utilizes to this day. When my wife or I was trying to help her accomplish something that she was sure she could do on her own, she would muster up all the power she could and confidently tell us, "Me self, not you self." You see, pride is our default position. It is essentially the idea that I am the center of my own personal universe. This, of course, leads to a whole lot of frustration when other people around us act like they are the center of the universe, and a simple examination of mathematics will tell you that there can only be one center to a universe. Just to make matters even more intolerable for a lot of people is the fact that the center position is already occupied. Since God created the universe and sustains it, He is what the universe is all about, and our frustration levels can go to absolute zero if we can ever fully accept that. The universe is for and about God, not us. "*The heavens declare the glory of God, and the sky proclaims the work of His hands. Day after day they pour out speech; night after night they communicate knowledge*" (Psalms 19:1–2).

The problem, though, is that I, in my natural state, want to be just like Satan. I want to be like the Most High (Isaiah 14:14). I want all of creation to declare that I exist and that I'm wonderful and worthy of being worshipped. I don't want any pain, have everything that I need, be in control of everything that happens, and have no equals. If I don't get that position, then I'll lie, cheat, steal, and murder to try to get there especially in avoiding the pain issue, and I'm not just talking about the physical stuff here either. Even more than physical pain, we really fear emotional pain because there is no antiseptic spray and Band-Aids that can deal with those wounds. So instead of believing in and trusting the God who is the actual center of the universe and who has declared what is right and wrong, our pride jumps up and says that we know better, so we have invented a little thing that's called situation ethics so that we can decide right and wrong to suit ourselves. And to bolster that concept, we often use a tragic situation that could (that's right, I wrote "could," not "will") hurt someone else. Then in the supposed name of someone else, our pride takes over, and we lie or cheat or steal or commit murder so that we can try to avoid some pain.

With pride as the core, then we see one of its uglier manifestations: evil conduct. Now for a lot of us, when we see the word *evil*, our minds picture things that shock our sensibilities. Things that we would never do like molesting a child or murdering six million Jews. While those things are definitely evil, there is more to it than that. The *Holman Bible Dictionary* defines evil as "that which is opposed to God and His purposes or that which, defined from human perspectives, is harmful and non-productive."[44] Evil, then, is *anything* that is opposed to God and what He is doing. The size or scope of the thing or how we view it isn't even a part of the equation. Evil is opposing God's view of what is right and wrong and choosing for ourselves what those are. Can you see the arrogant pride root in this one?

The other manifestation from the verse is perverse speech, and I think that takes a little defining as well. The Hebrew word for perverse is *tahpúkâh*[45] and carries the visual concept of something that is crooked or bent. Something that is not straight and true. Perverse speech, therefore, is the intentional distortion of that which is good and true, two things which are characteristics of God Himself. So again, because we fear that which we cannot control, then our response to the situation is commonly one of arrogant pride, and we say things that either just are not true or only have a veneer of truth covering. This is especially true when we run into the uncomfortable situations of life and we utilize the lie, often in the name of sparing someone else some level of pain, but usually it's just our pride welling up to try to avoid something that we don't want to face.

*　*　*　*　*

---

44. Trent C. Butler (general editor), *Holman Bible Dictionary* (Nashville, TN: Holman Bible Publishers, 1991), 447.
45. Strong's 8419.

Anytime that I took over a new squad or had an officer transfer onto my squad, I would lay out my expectations for the work performance that I expected to see. I also would inform them that police work is not an exact science and that I expected mistakes to happen. I also tried to reassure them that if they were following departmental policy and honestly trying to do the right thing in the right way, I would back them up with everything that I had. The only warning that I issued was "Just don't lie about it." With the exception of actual criminal conduct, most mistakes are survivable, even if the action is found to be outside of policy if they didn't lie about it. In that situation, there needs to be a high level of trust that your boss isn't out to get you any way that he can, and I always tried to foster that kind of trust. What some officers and people in general fail to grasp, though, is that trust is a two-way street. I needed to know that my officer was telling me the truth, especially when they messed up or when the situation turned out vastly different than they had intended. This was even truer when the officer had quite intentionally done something that he knew to be either wrong or completely outside of our department's policy. I am aware of more officers losing their career over lying than any other single activity.

But our pride tells us that we can say something that is crooked or bent, even if just slightly so, and we can control the situation and avoid the unpleasant outcomes that we envision that the truth will bring on. God says He hates that, and the Bible has a lot to say about lying since it identifies it as having been invented by Satan who is called *the father of lies* in John 8:44. In fact, the book of Revelation really drives home this point in 21:8 where it reads, "*But the cowards, unbelievers, vile, murderers, sexually immoral, sorcerers, idolaters, and all liars—their share will be in the lake that burns with fire and sulfur, which is the second death.*" Did you see that? Liars are lumped in with murderers, the sexually immoral, and cowards. The other thing that I need to point out here is that God's Word does not have levels of lying. There isn't any room for the so-called white lie. God is always straight and true, and therefore, He cannot tolerate anything that is not also completely true. But our fear and pride whisper that we're smarter. We can say something that isn't straight and true, and we'll be able to control the situation and the outcome.

Let's address that second verse now and really focus in on the second half, which says, *"A fool is hotheaded and yet feels secure."* Of course, the contrast is with a wise person, which is defined as one who *fears* (has reverential awe and respect) *the Lord and shuns evil.* We'll start off by defining just what a fool is. According to the online edition of the *Encarta Dictionary: English (North America)*,[46] a fool is either an unintelligent or ridiculous person. It also notes that it can be an offensive term for somebody with below-average intelligence or a psychiatric disorder. The Bible, though, has a much different definition, which is found in Psalms 14:1—*"The fool says in his heart, 'God does not exist.'"* A fool, therefore, is defined by what he or she believes and not on the basis of their ability to think or how silly they act.

As I was thinking over this section, I was remembering all the various hotheaded people and coworkers that I encountered over the course of my career. It was definitely the exception and not the rule that the hotheaded individual saw that his careless rage was responsible for the bad things happening around and to him. Invariably, they would instead blame everyone else for the results of their behavior with comments like "See what you made me do?" This was oftentimes really evident in domestic violence cases but could be observed in other situations as well. This careless raging is a tried-and-true tactic of those who like to bully and control others. They count on people being cowed by their raging to submit and give them their way and what they want. And in the world of domestic violence, that is most often the case with a physically bigger and stronger male over a smaller and weaker female.

One of my favorite stories came early in my career when my partner and I got dispatched to a priority call of a couple in the midst of a loud argument. When we arrived at the upstairs apartment, we could hear the shouting coming from inside. There was a small window beside the door, and I could see into the apartment but could

---

[46.] Accessed July 17, 2019.

not see the people involved. We knocked and announced ourselves, but initially there was no response, so we knocked a lot louder. At that moment, I saw the female resident run out from a back bedroom being pursued by a male in just his white underwear. The female had to go around their couch to get to the door, and when she did so, the male caught up to hear and violently pushed her into the wall where she collapsed. I relayed these events to my partner who was pounding on the door. Not knowing if the male was going to continue to assault the female, we made the decision to kick the door in and make an immediate entry. Unbeknownst to us, the hotheaded male had come around the couch to deal with whoever was banging on his door. It was at that exact moment that his door exploded as close to four hundred pounds of police officers came through it. The look of shock and surprise on his face is indelibly printed in my memory because about a half a second later, I tackled him and placed him under arrest.

And what precipitated his hotheaded raging where he lost control and slammed what we soon learned was his live-in girlfriend into the wall? A dispute over the use of a Santa Claus suit! We found out that she was the owner of the suit and had refused to let him wear it even though he had a paid gig to portray Santa at an event later that evening because of something that he had failed to do for her. So instead of apologizing and trying to work things out with his girlfriend, he chose to go the route of the hothead, with the final result being that he spent the night at the county jail in a set of county inmate coveralls since he arrived at the jail wearing only the same piece of clothing that he was arrested in. Although I never saw or heard from either half of this couple again, I've often wondered if at some point that night, he came to the realization that his hotheaded anger and frustration had brought him to this place or if instead he focused the blame on his girlfriend. The man in question undoubtedly felt very secure inside his apartment. All he could focus on was his rage at the audacity of his girlfriend to tell him no to something that he thought he needed. He could hear the irritating banging on his door but allegedly never heard the repeated shouts of "Phoenix Police! Open the door!" His handling of the dispute over the Santa suit with his girlfriend was foolish. And while I do not know whether or not he fit the biblical definition of a fool, I suspect that he did as nothing in his life (i.e., living with a girl before marriage, using physical violence on her) would give me any evidence to the contrary.

The Bible in Ephesians 5:25 tells men how they are supposed to treat their wives (hint: slamming them into a wall isn't there). That verse says, "*Husbands, love your wives, just as Christ loved the church and gave Himself for her.*" Did you catch that? Men are supposed to love their wives so much that they are willing to give up everything they have and be ready to die for their welfare. I can absolutely tell my male readers that if you love your wife to that level, you won't have any problems using the Santa suit they own. And even if for some reason she was to still tell you no, then that self-sacrificing love for her would get in the way of ever letting you get to the kind of hotheaded anger level that would cause her to run from you in fear and allow you to slam her into a nearby wall. Let's look now at the person that the fool is being contrasted with. First, let me note that the phrase "the Lord" is not in the original Hebrew, although some feel that it is implied based upon the context and the particular word for fear that was used. In the first part of Proverbs 14:6, the Bible asserts that a wise person has a reverential awe and respect and, therefore, shuns evil. The first part of that is, I think, relatively clear. If a person begins to have even a small understanding of just who God is and how powerful He is and wasn't just absolutely awestruck, then they probably would not be very wise indeed.

*   *   *   *   *

Imagine, for a moment if you will, coming face-to-face with the entity that created everything there is, including you, and responding with a yawn of indifference. And yet that is exactly what a myriad of people do when they look at the totality of all creation. For me anyway, I cannot think of a more unwise reaction. But it is the second part of what a wise person does that I want to key in on: the phrase "And shun evil." For some of us, the only vivid concept of shunning something or someone can be seen among certain very rigid religious groups that not only figuratively but literally turn their backs on one of their members if they are found to be in violation of the strict religious and societal rules that the community lives by. To shun something, therefore, is to intentionally avoid something or someone. It is to willfully have nothing to do with the thing or person being shunned. While that may be a formal practice within those religious groups, we all shun certain things or people in our lives to one degree or another.

When you are on a diet, you generally shun certain foods. You intentionally decide to have nothing to do with them. Those that are recovering from addiction will shun those things that will lead them back to the addiction and often times the places and the people that are associated with those things as well. And some of us shun people who are different than we are. They look different. They talk different. They live in a different socioeconomic level than we do. They worship differently, or they are involved in a sinful lifestyle that we disagree with. Any of these reasons and a host of others allow us, usually in a quiet and unstated way, to shun other people around us. The point is, we all tend to be involved in shunning in one fashion or another. But Scripture instructs us to shun evil as a natural by-product of fearing God.

A wise person who has reverential awe and respect should, as a natural outpouring of that attitude, intentionally avoid and have nothing to do with that which is evil. To my mind, that kind of makes logical sense. If I am that awestruck with God and have a reverential attitude that comes out of that, then I should want to intentionally avoid anything that He tells me is contrary to how good and pure that He is. The problem for most people here, though, is defining just what is evil. Although that should not really be a problem as it would be up to that entity that the wise person fears to define what evil is for us and fortunately, the Bible does just that and pretty darn definitively at that. But then pride jumps in, and we want to modify what those standards of evil are or outright deny them as actually existing at all. Or perhaps we go a different route and add things to the evil list that just are not biblical at all.

In the story of Eve and Satan as the serpent in the garden of Eden story from Genesis 3, Satan initiates a conversation with Eve about their dining options in the garden and asks her if it was true that they were not to eat from any of the trees. Eve correctly responded that they could eat from any of the tress except for the tree in the center. But then she added a prohibition, an evil activity if you will, that God had not stated. She said that they were not allowed to even touch that tree or they would die. She added something that God had not said. As far as we know, they could have sat on its branches or sat down on the ground and leaned against the tree or even just enjoyed the shade that it provided. They could have done all kinds of things in and around this tree, just not eat its fruit. But apparently, that evil activity list was not long enough, so Eve added one more. And that activity of adding to the prohibitions that God has given to us for our welfare and protection has continued on ever sense that time.

Before I go any further, let me define the word *evil* so that we all have the same understanding. For those in the Sunday school class that I teach, they will recognize that this is something I do a lot. I never want to assume that we all understand the meaning of a common term the same way because experience has taught me that we do not. This can lead to some really crazy misunderstandings.

So then what does the word *evil* mean? According to the *Holman Bible Dictionary*, evil is that which is opposed to God and His purposes or that which, defined from human perspectives, is "harmful and nonproductive."[47] Now let me contrast that with a more secular definition. The *Merriam-Webster* dictionary defines evil as something which is morally reprehensible, sinful, and wicked.[48] The problem with that, though, is who or what decides what is morally reprehensible. Any good student of history will tell you that the various activities which society deems as morally reprehensible are an ever-shifting set of standards. That is why I prefer to base the definition on God

---

[47.] Trent C. Butler (general editor), *Holman Bible Dictionary* (Nashville, TN: Holman Bible Publishers, 1991), 447.

[48.] https://www.merriam-webster.com/dictionary/evil.

and His purposes, which never change. So with that definition in mind, let's move on.

In the realm of Christendom, one can find an entire litany of added evils that cannot be found in the Bible, some of which have come and gone over time. But Christians are not alone in that activity. Judaism is rife with laws that have been added in the auspices of helping the faithful not break the actual commandments and laws found within Scripture. The problem is that, then, these added nonscriptural rules take on a level of requirement that makes them the equal of the actual commandments that God did give to people. Suddenly, or so it seems, being obedient to God's ordinances becomes a cumbersome job that requires the constant scrutiny of even the smallest of actions.

Shunning evil, or intentionally not having anything to do with the things that God has specifically prohibited, should be relatively simple and as natural an activity for the person who fears God as drinking water when you are thirsty. Moreover, it should be just as good for you as that proverbial glass of water is. It is only the foolish person who thinks that they can be a part of evil things while still maintaining a proper awe and respect for God. Jesus himself is quoted as saying that a person cannot serve two masters (Matthew 6:24). But the foolish person goes right on trying or decides to just have no fear of God at all and just embrace those things that God has expressly prohibited. This makes me think of that oft-quoted cliché that repeating the same activity but expecting a different result is the definition of insanity.

I saw the wise person concept lived out in the lives of a number of different people that I have had the honor of knowing. I know or have known both men and women who had such an awe and reverence for God that they just quite naturally shunned all the evil that existed around them. One of them, and one of my mentors, was a man by the name of Lew Lawton. He was an associate pastor at a church that I attended and knew more about the Bible than I can ever hope to achieve. While his life was extremely godly, I never knew him to focus on an exhaustive list of thou-shalt-nots. Instead, his focus was always on the awesomeness of who God is and that in a right relationship with Him, there would be neither room nor desire for the things that God wanted us to avoid. Now that is not to say that if someone was going down a wrong road, he wouldn't step in to correct their path. That's just exactly what a loving person would do for those that he was responsible for. But it was never about the rules; it was always about getting back to the right relationship with God through submitting to the lordship of Jesus Christ.

August

This month, we will look at two more Hebrew words that are translated into our word *fear*. Both of them come from the book of Job. Then we will finish with one additional fear reference.

> Did I fear a great multitude, or did the contempt of families terrify me, that I kept silence and went not out of the door? (Job 31:34 KJV)

The word for fear here is *ârats*[49] and carries the concept of dreading something to the point that you are actually shaking. The word is best understood in conjunction with the word for *terrify*, which is *châthath*,[50] which has the initial meaning of prostrate but not as a means of respect. It is to be so scared that you hit the floor shaking and unable to move or fight back. Essentially the imagery here is fear to the point that your natural fight-or-flight reaction is so overwhelmed that you can't do anything but lay there and shake as you await whatever caused this level of fear to complete the event.

For those of you who may not be familiar with the story of Job, the Bible depicts him as a well-to-do man who has great faith in God. Satan (his name means "adversary") comes before God, presumably to accuse mankind of the same rejection that he was guilty of, and God points out that Job was a righteous man. Satan believes that it is only because that Job has great wealth both in the terms of large herds and flocks but also with several children who are apparently grown up and doing well. Satan asks for, and receives permission

---

49. Strong's 6206.
50. Strong's 2865.

to, attack everything that Job has in the belief that then Job will turn away from God. Subsequently, Job loses both his way of life (his flocks and herds) and then the lives of his children. This is significant because in a time before social welfare concepts, the elderly depended on their children to take care of them when they were old. When those attacks did not produce the results that Satan thought he would get, he supposes that Job would falter if his life was in jeopardy. He makes this case to God and this time is given permission to attack Job directly with the caveat that he cannot kill him. And so now to compound the sorrow at the loss of his livelihood and the lives of his children, he finds himself covered in boils. The pain and discomfort had to have been excruciating. His wife cracks under the pressure and says, *"Do you still retain your integrity? Curse God and die!"* (Job 2:9). Then three of his friends come to visit him and try to figure out the age-old question of why bad things happen to good people. It is in the midst of those discussions with Job that we find this verse about fear.

Essentially, the argument has been made to Job that he must have some grievous sin in his life. What his friend has proposed is a variant on the ancient concept of karma. If you do good things in life, then generally you should expect good things to happen to you. If you do evil things, then you should expect that bad things will happen to you. While I realize that they were trying to understand something and make sense of it all, what they were essentially doing was denying the presence of God as an active controller of the universe that He created. Job answers their supposition of deep sin in his life in the form of a question. He asks them if he ever appeared to be afraid of all the people around him (the multitude) or if he was ever apparently terrified in dealing with the other family clans around. If he had been aware of any great and especially awful sins, then he would not have led the open and public life in the community that he did prior to the calamities that had recently occurred. He would have been afraid of their reaction to his evil life. So he uses his own life to deny the charge of his friends and points out that his lifestyle prior to these tragedies belied any knowledge of sin on his part.

This kind of fear—"paralyzing, unable to move, or think clearly" fear—is a very real thing. It can be especially true if our conscience is fueling the fear. My favorite story about that kind of fear is the quote from Mark Twain when he wrote, "I once sent a dozen of my friends a telegram saying 'Flee at once—all is discovered.' They all left town immediately." For the men and women in my former profession of law enforcement, though, that kind of fear can also lead to real unexpected danger.

The scenario goes something like this. You are driving a marked patrol car in your regular patrol area at night when you see a car operating with only one headlight. It's a quiet night as far as radio calls for service go, so you decide to stop the driver and let him know that he needs to get it fixed. What you don't know is that he has just killed his girlfriend after a heated dispute over his dalliances with another girl. As he pulls over, his conscience is screaming at him, and he believes that you know what he's done, and now he begins to prepare himself to defend his life and get away even if he doesn't know exactly where that is. As you walk up to have a simple conversation with the driver, his fear has risen to the explosive level, and you are about to be in a fight for your life over a one-headlight violation. On any other day and time, this same driver would probably have been very receptive and extremely grateful that all he got was a verbal warning about the headlight. Conscience-driven fear can make us unable to think (move mentally), but Job, in talking to his friends, pointed out that this had not been his issue at all. He knew his life to be blameless because he had dealt with whatever had happened in his past and his actions verified that.

The thing about this kind of fear is that it is always lurking down deep in our minds. Really, this is just another version of fear of the unknown. Our imagination fills in the unknown void with all kinds of disasters that we think may befall us if others are to learn the truth. While some of them may very well be based in some reality, generally our minds tend to overstate the outcome. We can go years with that event safely tucked away in our minds until something brings it back into the light, and then suddenly the fear can be as real and debilitating as the first moments after the event when your conscience was screaming, "You've really messed up this time! You won't get away with it! Your life is over!" The only way to deal with these latent fear bombs in our minds is to bring them out into the light of day. Yes, that is going to be uncomfortable, but more often than not, the results of dealing with whatever issue your conscience is generating fear about is far less than our imagination has led us to believe it would be. I cannot begin to recount all the times that I was questioning a suspect who would visibly relax after they admitted what they had done. In fact, it was often the case that the bigger the crime, the more relaxed the subject would be after they had admitted to the crime, and now they could just deal with the real consequences and stop worrying about the imagined ones.

Now for the really great news, we can eliminate this kind of fear at any time. All we have to do is to confess what we've done. That confession begins with God. Scripture tells us that if we will do this, God *"is faithful and righteous to forgive us our sins and to cleanse us from all unrighteousness"* (1 John 1:9). But confession doesn't always stop there; sometimes we have to confess to other believers. James 5:16 says, *"Therefore confess your sins to each other and pray for each other so that you may be healed. The prayer of a righteous man has great power to prevail."* Now just to be clear, this verse is from a passage that is talking about the prayer of faith. But notice that this prayer is supported by confessing where we've messed up to other believers. Now that can be very scary since people aren't like God. They are not always faithful. They may repeat something that shouldn't be repeated. They may forget what Jesus referred to as one of the two greatest commandments: to *love your neighbor as you love yourself.* They may in fact act in a very unloving way. But I don't see any caveats in the James 5:16 verse. It doesn't say if they've first proven themselves to be trustworthy. And the reason that I think that no qualifiers are put in this verse is because confession isn't about others; it's about you. It's about getting that thing out into the light of day where it can be dealt with. It's about agreeing with God that what you did was wrong and then not having the guilt of that event hold you hostage in the fear that it's going to be discovered.

How many of us have something in our past, the proverbial skeleton in the closet, that we keep carefully locked away? By doing this, we're effectively saying that we're the only one who knows about it, but since God is both omnipresent (everywhere all the time) and omniscient (knows everything), then who are we fooling by staying hostage to something that God already knows about? Eliminate this kind of fear. Confess and be done with it because God is faithful.

*   *   *   *   *

Upon earth there is not his like, who is made without fear. (Job 41:33)

The next word for fear that we discover in the book of Job is *chath*,[51] which means to be crushed or broken. It is derived from *châthath*,[52] which means to be broken down into a prostrated position by either violence or confusion and fear. This verse is in the midst of a long four-chapter speech by God Himself to Job as He speaks from a whirlwind after Job has debated with his friends as to the whys of his predicament and the nature of God. God is going to set the record straight.

All of Job chapter 41 is devoted to the description of a giant water creature called Leviathan. There is a lot of speculation as to just what this creature is, but I'm not going to enter into that debate here because it is of no consequence to this topic. Rather, I would direct you to read Job 34, as God describes this untamable (verse 5) and fearsome creature that none of mankind's weapons at the time (sword, spear, dart, arrow, slingstones, or clubs) would have any effect on (verses 26–29). God points out, though, that even this unstoppable creature belongs to Him (verse 11). God then finishes His description by telling Job that this creature is so at the top of the food chain that it is without fear. Leviathan is not crushed or broken or subservient to anything else, especially man. This creature is so

---

[51.] Strong's 2844.
[52.] Strong's 2865.

secure in his power that he has no worries at all. That kind of consistent fearlessness across all fronts is rare in the animal kingdom and virtually nonexistent in humans. Of course, there is a lot of anecdotal evidence that suggests that some people are capable of that level of fearlessness for a short while. The Bible also has its share of stories about people acting without fear. Perhaps the best known of those is the teenage David taking on the heavily armored and well-trained giant Goliath. In fact, not only was he not afraid of a vastly superior enemy, he was also completely confident that he would beat Goliath, and so he ran at him across an open battlefield armed with nothing more than a sling and some smooth stones (1 Samuel 17:48). Later in his life, though, David made a number of fear-based decisions that had disastrous results.

When we see someone who seems to be absolutely fearless all the time, we know that it is often just a front that they project to the world around them. I have had situations where I've dealt with some of the toughest, fearless criminals you can imagine when they're in view of others, especially their peers and associates. Those same tough guys, though, when I had them alone in an interview room, would often break down in tears as the bravado and the false fearlessness fell away. Occasionally, I would see that same fearless facade on a young officer. I knew that trying to maintain that show for his peers was impossible in the long run, not to mention that it could turn out to be pretty psychologically damaging when the truth came out. My encouragement to officers who were engaged in that type of behavior was to let them know that we are all afraid to one degree or another and that a little well-managed fear was actually a good thing because it usually keeps us from doing something incredibly stupid. Expressing concern over the potential hazards in a situation wasn't a sign of weakness; it just showed that the necessary self-preservation process was intact. As police officers, we didn't deny our fear nor were we devoid of normal fear; we just learned to manage it to get to a resolution of the situation.

There are some people who are truly lacking in any fear response, but that is due to a medical condition. According to Radiopedia.

org, Urbach-Wiethe disease is a very rare condition.[53] Among other things, it progressively destroys the amygdala, the almond-shaped part of the brain that researchers believe is the anatomical seat of fear.[54] Essentially, then, the few hundred people globally who have been diagnosed with this condition have a portion of their brain that isn't functioning correctly, so they don't process a normal fear response in almost any situation. This, of course, can make decision-making somewhat problematic especially when a correct response to a given situation may be to flee or fight for your life.

People can be as fearless as Leviathan when they know they have the right protection and when they know they are protected against any weapon that may come against them, then fear is no longer a part of the equation. The prophet Isaiah, in giving God's Word about the future glory of the nation of Israel, said this: "*No weapon formed against you will succeed, and you will refute any accusation raised against you in court. This is the heritage of the LORD's servants, and their righteousness is from Me.*" This is the LORD's declaration" (Isaiah 54:17). Can you imagine that? Being impervious to any weapon is beyond imagination.

I used to be a big superhero comic book fan, especially the DC world of Superman, Batman, and all the other superheroes that made up the Justice League of America. The only thing, though, was that each of these heroes had a vulnerability or two. That vulnerability was something that an enemy could weaponize to either defeat the hero (temporarily of course) or to neutralize their superpower and make them just a normal person. When these were depicted on television, real human vulnerabilities would sometime sneak into the program. For instance, in the old black-and-white Superman show, he would stand there motionless as the bad guys would shoot at him until they ran out of bullets. But then when they threw their gun at him, he would duck. That was because the bullets had been added on

---

53. Accessed March 28, 2020, https://radiopaedia.org/articles/urbach-wiethe-disease.
54. Accessed March 28, 2020, https://healthland.time.com/2013/02/11/how-to-terrify-the-fearless/.

to the film, but when the bad guy threw a very real prop gun at the actor portraying Superman, he wisely ducked out of the way.

But let me get back to my point. According to God's Word, we can be absolutely fearless as Leviathan because no weapon that man can devise will succeed in taking us out of God's hand. Can our human body be destroyed? Of course it can. There is a whole host of martyrs down through history that can attest to that. But those weapons can't do two very important things. First, they can't kill our eternal souls, the essence and reality of who we are. Our bodies are only temporary housing for our souls, and they were doomed to eventually die anyway, so human weapons can't do anything more than what time was already in the process of doing from the moment we were created in our mother's womb. Second, human weapons—many of which now are far more devastating than mere swords, clubs, and slingstones—cannot remove those of us who've been adopted into God's family through faith in the life, death, and resurrection of Jesus from God's hand. Through the prophet Isaiah, God tells His people to not be afraid for this very reason—God's hand is holding us. Isaiah 41:10 says, *"Do not fear, for I am with you; do not be afraid, for I am your God. I will strengthen you; I will help you; I will hold on to you with My righteous right hand."* If that's true, then what human weapon, as incredibly destructive as some of them are, can harm me? What virus or disease can destroy me? None of those things can touch me; they can only complete the job that time was already in the process of doing to this temporary physical shell.

Let me finish off this section by looking at the wording in Isaiah 41:10. To begin with, notice that it begins with a directive to not be involved in fear. But this isn't just to be a case of super positive thinking; it's because God is with us. God reiterates that we're not to be afraid, and this time, He adds it's because He's our personal God. He's not some impersonal force or a disinterested big-picture god. He is my God. He is your God, and His promise is that He will hold on to you and that you are in His hand. What power can possible remove you from that position? Is there anything someone can do to break the grip of God's hand on you? Is there anything you can do that would force God to let go of you? Remember, He's omniscient.

He already knows everything, so there's not some sin in your future that He doesn't already know about. You are not powerful enough to remove yourself from God's hand!

*　　*　　*　　*　　*

> Put them in fear, O LORD, That the nations may know themselves to be but men. (Psalms 9:20 NKJV)

The word translated as fear in this verse is *môwrâ*,[55] which comes from the word *yârê*[56] that we've already seen implies reverence. This word, though, has more of the idea of a fearful thing or deed that causes someone to dread what is coming to the point of being terrified. Go back and read that verse again but this time with a better understanding of just what David is asking God to do. As I am writing this, the entire globe is in a state of fear from a pandemic that has touched every nation to one extent or another. In spite of all the combined wealth and military prowess around the world, the nations have learned that in the face of something as small as a virus, they are just men and just as capable of dying as the next man from something that they are essentially powerless to control.

This verse is the culmination of a Davidic psalm where he celebrates God's justice in his life. He begins the psalm by thanking God for everything that He's done for him and then acknowledges that when his enemies were not able to destroy him, it wasn't his doing but God's. When you know that you have someone as big and powerful as God Himself in your corner, that can make you absolutely fearless. To fully understand this verse, though, I think you need to back up to verse 19, which reads, *"Rise up, Lord! Do not let mere humans prevail; let the nations be judged in your presence."* David is asking for God to assert Himself and to not allow mere humans to think that they are in control. He wants the nations to be judged for

---

[55.] Strong's 4172.
[56.] Strong's 3372.

their failure to follow God's laws and acknowledge Him as the ruler of creation. It's only then that we see how that is to be accomplished through dread to the point of being terrified as the nations learn how completely helpless they actually are.

Pride, the core DNA in all sin, is a very strong motivator. Even in the grip of worldwide fear, mankind would rather not acknowledge God as Lord because they would rather believe that they are the lords of their own lives. That they can control their own destiny and decide for themselves what is right and wrong. They still desperately want to believe the lie that Satan told Eve back in the garden of Eden when he said that she wouldn't die if she ate the fruit that God had forbidden to be eaten. So instead of humbling themselves before God and depending upon their own wisdom, nations maintain their pride and watch and mourn as people die.

I have seen that kind of dread and terror a few times in my career, and it is something to see as a person completely breaks down because they know they are powerless to stop what is coming or what they think is coming at them. On one particular evening, I arrested a young gang-banger from the Los Angeles area who was visiting friends in Arizona. He had instigated a minor disturbance and then had punched another guy, so I took him into custody for a misdemeanor assault charge. Because he didn't have his identification with him and because he wasn't local, I couldn't just issue him a summons and send him back to his relative's home. He had to be booked into jail for the night. When I placed the handcuffs on him, he was still fairly defiant and keeping up the show of being a tough-as-nails LA gangster. After I got in the car and pulled away from the scene, he was much more compliant as he asked me what was going to happen to him. I explained the entire process step by step and he visibly relaxed. A few moments later, though, that same young man who had been so easygoing after getting his explanation was now completely freaking out in the backseat of my patrol car. Up to that point, I had never seen that kind of unchecked and absolute terror.

The particular route that I took to the station led me through a section of town that was a light industrial area of warehouses and small storefront businesses. Being that it was late in the evening, it was pretty much deserted. As we began to drive through this area, my prisoner began demanding to know where we were going. I repeated the plan and kept driving, but each second as we drove deeper into this nighttime ghost town, he became more and more afraid as he asked over and over again what was going to happen to him. He was thrashing about so much that I stopped my car, and then the complete terror hit him as he began to cower against one door and started sobbing about how sorry he was and that he didn't mean it. I was completely flabbergasted by what was taking place and tried to reassure him that he was going to be all right. I quickly realized that this wasn't working and decided to just hurry on to the station and get him out of my car where I would have more light and other officers to help me. Then as we left the industrial area and got on to the freeway, the young man began to slightly calm down as he looked around while still asking where we were going and what was going to happen to him. I again repeated the plan and hurried on to the station.

When we pulled through the security gate into the parking lot, I told him that we had arrived, and now he finally began to relax and got quiet. After I walked him into the station, removed the handcuffs, and placed him into a holding cell, I asked him what had freaked him out so badly. He told me that in the part of LA where he was from, if the cops took you to a deserted area like that industrial park at night, you weren't going to jail. You were going to get a severe beating or possibly worse. At that point, I reassured him that everything was going to go the exact the way I had originally told him it would, and from that point on, I had nothing but cooperation. Now I don't know if this young man had first-hand knowledge of this sort of "beat and release" or if it was just repeated rumor among his fellow gangsters. Either way, he believed it to be true, and so the dread and terror that he experienced was very real. It was just a few years later that the Rampart Division scandal broke, and I always wondered about what that young man had told me.

That young man knew that being a gangster meant nothing when he was in the hands of law enforcement, and he was completely terrified. At some point, I hope that David's request is answered, and that fear may drive the nations of this world to admit that they are only human and in need of the Lord of all to deliver them.

SEPTEMBER

This month, we are going back to the New Testament to look at three verses about fear and being afraid and the nuances that we can find in them. Here is the first one.

> For rulers are not a terror to good works, but to the evil. Wilt thou then not be afraid of the power? Do that which is good, and thou shalt have praise of the same: For he is the minister of God to thee for good. But if thou do that which is evil, be afraid; for he beareth not the sword in vain: for he is the minister of God, a revenger to execute wrath upon him that doeth evil. (Romans 13:3–4 KJV)

We'll start off this month by looking at what Paul wrote to the Roman believers on how not to be afraid and why. Paul wrote this letter about AD 57 while he was in Corinth on his last trip back to Jerusalem to deliver an offering for the poor Jewish believers that he had collected from the gentile churches he had founded.[57] To put it in even more of a historical context, Nero was the current emperor of Rome, and while at this point the overt hostility and persecution of Christians that would come to mark Nero's later years had not fully begun, Nero's reputation for evil and death that we can read and study about today was already being forged in the fires of his personal narcissism.

---

[57] Introduction to Romans in *CSB Spurgeon Study Bible* (Nashville, TN: Homan Bible Publishers, 2017), 1,511.

Paul had just completed thoughts on Christian ethics in the latter part of chapter 12, but now he shifted gears completely as he addressed a Christian's relation to the government that he or she lived under. This is a fairly basic axiom that if you are not breaking the law, the enforcers of the law pose no threat. Of course, that is assuming that there is no capricious harassment due to some form of bias. But generally speaking, if you are following the directives of the law, you have absolutely nothing to fear when law enforcement is on the scene. Of course, if you have been up to something, that changes matters entirely, and there should be some level of fear. The next verse agrees with that assessment when it says, "*For government is God's servant for your good. But if you do wrong, be afraid, because it does not carry the sword for no reason. For government is God's servant, an avenger that brings wrath on the one who does wrong.*" Did you catch what it said there, "*If you do wrong, be afraid*"? The government is in place to bring God's wrath on the one who does wrong.

Now I'm going to let you in on a little secret. Police officers are terrible mind readers. We have to depend on one or more of our normal five senses to tell us if someone is doing something inappropriate or illegal. Suspects, though, always seemed to assume that I knew what they were up to or what they had just done. Even though I didn't know, oftentimes the fear that they manifested told me that they obviously did. This is so common, in fact, that we had a term for it when we would drive up and suddenly one or more individuals started making a very quick exit. We call it felony running. Felony running is not a crime by the way. It was just a person who was living out verse 4 above. They knew what they had done, and so when I arrived on the scene, their fear of being arrested convinced them that the only course of action they had was to run and try to get away. Most of the time, they were very successful in running away from me, as I had no idea why they were running in the first place. Usually I would sit there in my patrol car somewhat bemused watching someone doing everything they could to get away even though no one was chasing them. This often brought another verse to mind. Proverbs 28:1 says, "*The wicked flee when no one is pursuing them, but the righteous are as bold as a lion.*" Knowing that this was written over

2,500 years ago tells me that what many other police officers and I have witnessed is not a new phenomenon.

The Greek word for *afraid* in the verse from Romans is *phŏbĕō*, from which we get our word *phobia*.[58] The people that the writer of the proverb you just read that were written about and the people that I observed engaging in felony running had either just done something or, while in the midst of doing their nefarious act, knew better. Additionally, either because of past experiences, the experience of friends and/or relatives or just from having watched numerous cop shows, they had a very powerful fear and dislike of facing the consequences for their actions. They didn't want to go to jail, stand trial, and have the whole world know what they had done, and so they ran for all they were worth. Many of us experience that same kind of fear from time to time, but generally, we react differently. The place that many of us experience this sort of fear is while driving. It happens right when you look in your rearview mirror, and suddenly there is a motorcycle cop right behind you that just seemed to appear out of nowhere. Or you see a marked unit sitting off the side of the roadway facing the road so that they can pull out whenever they need to. Most of us get that sudden flash of fear and the thought of "Oh no" races through our brain as we instinctively let off the gas, and some of us actually touch the brakes even if we aren't exceeding the speed limit at that precise moment.

Why do we do that? Generally, it's because most of us (me too) do not consistently obey all the traffic laws to the letter. Those minor infractions often come with a good dose of rationalization like "I'm just keeping up with traffic" or "This is the high-speed lane; you're supposed to go faster" or "I was almost stopped, but there was an opening, so I had to go to make my turn safely." We all took the written driving test and knew better, but most of us rationalize away our sloppy driving habits until that set of red and blue lights suddenly appears. Then our conscience screams "You've been caught!" and the fear of getting stopped, losing another ten minutes when we're already running late and getting an expensive ticket take

---

[58] Strong's 5399.

over. Of course, that gets compounded many times over if you have some unpaid tickets already or a suspended driver's license or, even worse, a warrant out for your arrest from something else. I have had a number of people suddenly speed off and then try to engage in a game of vehicular hide-and-seek, which of course got my undivided attention. After the game was done and we were having a discussion (usually they were seated in the back seat of my car for these chats), they would tell me that they thought their license was suspended or that they had a warrant. I found that it was just about fifty-fifty as to whether or not it was in fact the case. You see, they knew that they hadn't paid a previous ticket or that they failed to obey a judge's directives from a previous incident, so now when they saw the police, they were afraid and drove away.

Some of you may be wondering about what happened to those who didn't have a suspended driver's license or a warrant that ran and subsequently got caught. Well, depending on just what transpired during the hide-n-seek phase, I generally made sure that they had a little something to remember their escapade with and the knowledge that had they merely not sped off in the first place, I probably wouldn't have even noticed them.

Let's get back to the verses, though, as they explain how to not be afraid in the first place. Paul's question to the Christians there in Rome was "*Do you not want to be afraid of the authorities?*" then "*Do what is good, and you will have its approval.*" You don't have to be afraid of a man or woman in a police uniform *if* you are doing what you're supposed to be doing in the manner that you're supposed to be doing it. This kind of fear is all too often a product of our own reasoning as to why the rules don't apply to us or to the particular situation we're in. The problem of course, though, is that they do, and we know it. We just want to disregard them for our own convenience.

> But even if you should suffer for righteousness, you are blessed. Do not fear what they fear or be disturbed. (1 Peter 3:14)

This verse from the apostle Peter uses the same Greek word for fear as the Romans passage you just read about. Peter's message is also somewhat similar to that of Paul to the Roman church, as he is also talking about doing the right thing despite what circumstances a Christian finds themselves in. He also begins with the same general supposition in the preceding verse when he says, *"And who will harm you if you are deeply committed to what is good?* (1 Peter 3:13). Thus, both apostles make the same general assumption that if you are obeying the law, then the law will take no notice of you. Peter, though, makes a really phenomenal statement in verse 14 when he says, *"But even if you should suffer for righteousness, you are blessed."* He then quotes a passage from Isaiah 8:12 when he says, *"Do not fear what they fear or be disturbed."* So let me break this down for you into some understandable morsels for you to chew on.

First off, he reverses our normal way of thinking and says that if you should suffer for doing the right thing, at the right time, and in the right way, you are blessed. To be blessed means that you are happy. A person who is to be envied for what they have received. Now I don't know anyone that I can think of who looks at a fellow Christian who is suffering and says, "Wow, how lucky they are! They must be really happy that this is happening to them." In fact, it's all too common to speculate as to why they are suffering and to wonder what was in their life that God was dealing with. Of course, the moment that we entertain those kinds of thoughts, we have become just like Job's three so-called friends and put the blame squarely on the shoulders of the one suffering. Before I go too much further, though, we have to figure out what Peter meant when he said "suffer" in this passage. What I think of as suffering and what you do may be vastly different, and I'm pretty sure that our ideas are different yet from a believer Christian currently living in Pakistan. In this letter, Peter uses that word a number of times, so if we examine them, we should get a pretty clear picture of what he meant here. So let's look at a few of them to learn just what kind of suffering can leave us blessed.

The first time it shows up is in 1 Peter 2:21 when it says that *"Christ suffered for you, leaving you an example, that you should fol-*

low in His steps." So right off the bat, Peter is referencing the suffering that Jesus endured up to and including His crucifixion. That's a pretty high bar, and we haven't even considered the other three. All too often, I think of suffering as having to drive somewhere during the summer heat when my air conditioning in the car isn't working. I don't think of it as being whipped, beaten beyond recognition, and then nailed to a cross.

Next up is 1 Peter 3:17 where Peter writes, *"For it is better to suffer for doing good, if that should be God's will, than for doing evil."* So the picture is starting to come into focus on what Peter meant by suffering. As an eye witness, Peter noted in 1 Peter 2:23 that when Jesus was suffering, that *"when He was reviled, He did not revile in return; when He was suffering, He did not threaten but entrusted Himself to the One who judges justly."* Jesus then becomes the best example of suffering for doing good.

Next up is 1 Peter 4:1 where Peter states that Jesus suffered in the flesh. It was a very physical thing that is really beyond our ability to understand. I think that Mel Gibson's movie *Passion of the Christ* graphically gives us a bit of what Jesus suffered in the flesh. Although let me insert a warning here. If you have not seen this film and intend to, the physical suffering is extremely graphic and not for the faint of heart or young children to observe.

Peter concludes his concept of suffering in this letter by telling us what we shouldn't be suffering for. 1 Peter 4:15 reads, *"None of you, however, should suffer as a murderer, a thief, an evildoer, or a meddler."* That's quite the list, especially when you consider that being a meddler (one who gets involved in other people's business uninvited) is put on the same level with being a murderer and a thief. Now I understand what a murderer is (I got to meet a few of them up close and personal), and a thief covers the gamut from taking a single candy bar from the store up to those so-called white-collar criminals who bilk millions from their employer, their clients, or unsuspecting and foolish people through various scams. I even have a pretty good idea what a meddler is, as I've had those types try to insert themselves into my life on numerous occasions. But what does Peter mean by an evildoer? That word in the original Greek is *kakŏpŏiŏs*,[59] which is a compound word from a word that means to intentionally do something and a word that means worthless, depraved, or injurious. Thus, an evildoer is someone who intentionally does something that is worthless, immoral, or corrupt, and that hurts others. And yep, I had an entire career of dealing with the evildoers in our midst.

So Peter's point, then, in his letter is that Christians should expect to suffer, and perhaps pretty severely, because after all Jesus got the death penalty for doing good deeds. But Christians shouldn't be suffering for hurting others either physically or financially. This is especially true when you consider that Jesus said that the second of the greatest commandments was to love your neighbor as yourself (Matthew 22:37–40). So now that we've got the suffering thing covered, let's get to the second part of our key verse for this section, which says, *"Do not fear what they fear or be disturbed."* What do they fear and get disturbed by that I'm not supposed to get all worked up over? This is a book about fear and how and why to not participate in it, so we need to get this right as well.

You'll recall that I told you that Peter was quoting from Isaiah 8:12. In that passage, the prophet Isaiah was talking to the faithful people in the southern kingdom of Judah, and he told them to not follow the lead of some of their countrymen who were living in dread of possible attacks that were coming from Syria and their fellow Jews in the apostate country of Israel. But at the time of Peter's letter, those weren't the issues, so it had to be something related since he quoted Isaiah from that earlier time in history. In this passage, the persons are not named; but in looking at the totality of what Peter is writing about, they cannot be enemies who try to harm Christians like the people of Syria and Israel were threatening to do. Like in Isaiah's time, Peter was warning against becoming afraid like some fellow Christians who, for fear of man and circumstances around them, were beginning to abandon Christianity. Peter is, then, really saying in this passage to not follow those who become afraid because of what others may do to them and turn their backs on their faith.

[59.] Strong's 2555.

King David said it well when he started Psalm 27 with "*The LORD is my light and my salvation—whom should I fear? The LORD is the stronghold of my life—of whom should I be afraid?*" But how often do we give into herd mentality here? If others are afraid, then we can catch that fear like one catches a virus that spreads from one person to the next, and Peter tells us, in no uncertain terms, to not do that. We serve the same Lord as David, and we need to incorporate that level of confidence in Him that I don't need to fear anyone. Will I suffer at times, even unto death? Yes, but if I do, I need to make sure that like Jesus, it's because I was doing all the good and righteous things that I could. Then if God allows me the privilege of suffering to a degree like Jesus did, I know that ultimately it will be for my own good as the promise of Romans 8:28 ("*We know that all things work together for the good of those who love God: those who are called according to His purpose*") assures me.

The third verse that I want to examine this month is from what is commonly referred to as the heroes of faith in Hebrews chapter 11, specifically 11:23:

> By faith, after Moses was born, he was hid-
> den by his parents for three months, because they
> saw that the child was beautiful, and they didn't
> fear the king's edict.

As you've probably deduced by now, the emphasis in this chapter is fear in relationship to the government; and in this verse, we're going to take a slightly different, albeit related, tact than we've already gone through. The issue here is when, and under what circumstances, should a Christian disobey the government and not be afraid of the consequences. So for those of you who don't know the story, the Pharaoh (like a king) of Egypt decides that all the male children born to the Israelites were to be killed since the people were multiplying and he was afraid that they would join with Egypt's enemies and destroy the country from within. He had already moved them into a slave status but wanted only a generation of females so that there wouldn't be any males to fight against him. When we read the story in Exodus chapter 2, it only mentions Moses's mother, but now in Hebrews we see that both his parents were involved in the decision to defy the Pharaoh's edict. It was only his mother that carried out the plan, perhaps to not draw attention, but we don't really know why.

So if God is perfect, then His commands are perfect and apply to all people in all times in all situations. If they didn't, then by definition they wouldn't be perfect and neither would God. With this in mind, we read in a lot of places that we are to obey the government (Romans 13:1–14, Hebrews 13:17, 1 Peter 2:1–25, and Titus 3:1, just to name a few). So the question then arises, When should (notice I didn't say can) a Christian disobey the government and, like Moses's parents, not be afraid to do so?

Like the old bracelets from the 1990s, we first need to ask "What would Jesus do?" or, even better, look at His life and see what He did and didn't do. At the time of Jesus's ministry, the nation Israel was under the oppressive control of Rome. The Jews were looking and hoping for a messiah that would lead them out of foreign control and back to being a regional power like in the days of David and Solomon. But Jesus did not call for revolution against Rome, even though it was an oppressive conqueror of God's chosen people. In fact, He directly taught that the taxes that Rome imposed were to be paid (Mark 12: 13–17). On the other hand, the apostles refused to obey an order from the government in Israel not to preach and teach in Jesus's name (see Acts 5:27–29). The difference between the two is that one impacts what God has commanded and the other does not. The principle here, then, is whenever the government says that Christians cannot do the things that God has commanded us to do or conversely tells us to do things He has commanded us not to do, it is then, and only then, that we stand upon very solid ground in disobeying the government.

In the early 1960s, a psychological test was conducted to see how much authority people would be obedient to or accept without question. The subjects were placed at a set of controls behind a one-way mirror, while on the other side of the mirror was a man who was strapped to a machine that appeared to administer electrical shocks. An authoritative person in a white coat directed these test subjects to press a button that would inflict pain on the subject. As the experiment continued, they were instructed to turn up the dials on the machine to even higher levels of shock as the man strapped to the machine continued to scream in pain. The person in the white coat, who was the authority figure, continued to tell the people to push the lever higher, and most continued to do so until the subject seemed to be either in a state of collapse or dead. Though the subject gave every evidence of being in excruciating pain, people obeyed orders to hurt him, simply because those orders came from an authority figure. Only a few people resisted orders to inflict pain. The rest of them did as they were told to do (see the Milgram Shock Experiment).

*   *   *   *   *

To bring this month to a general conclusion, then, if we don't want to be afraid, we should be constantly focused on doing good, living righteously, and obeying the government and the laws it provides because they are designed for our peace and welfare. We are only to stand in opposition to the government and its human representatives when those directives or laws directly oppose what the Bible teaches us to do or to refrain from doing. But even then, that opposition should be the last alternative, not the first thing that we turn to.

As I'm writing this, the US (and the rest of the world) is starting to come out of the restrictions and lockdowns that were required by the various states to try to combat the spread of a particularly nasty coronavirus by the common name of COVID-19. Because my country is made up of a collection of semi-independent states that are banded together under a federal government, the response has been different depending on which state you lived in. Some states opted to go with some of the most extreme and draconian mandates, which included criminal penalties for noncompliance, while others elected to go with a softer hand with strongly encouraged suggestions for social distancing, mask wearing, sanitizing, and other preventative measures. Most states, though, fell somewhere along a line between these two polar responses. Christians lived in each of these states and had to really look at what it meant, in a very practical way, to determine what their response would be to a sudden change in how they conducted their day-to-day life.

For many, the most troubling aspect was the almost overnight cessation of being able to gather together for weekly services. Additionally, depending upon the traditions of your denomination, there were weddings scheduled to occur, funerals to be conducted, and infant or adult baptisms that needed to be completed. Add to that mix the biblical directive from Hebrews 10:25 to *"not forsaking the assembling of ourselves together, as is the manner of some, but exhorting one another, and so much the more as you see the Day approaching"* (NKJV). Along with the biblical mandate to regularly get together with other believers, the First Amendment to the Constitution starts out with "Congress shall make no law respecting an establishment of religion, or *prohibiting the free exercise thereof.*"[60] So what is a Christian to do?

Some pastors decided to openly oppose the directives to not have their church open based upon the two issues that I just listed. Others elected to comply and completely shut down and waited for their individual state government to tell them when they could resume operations. Most, though, got very creative and found new ways to obey both the government directives and the biblical mandate. Things like having a drive-in service where people stayed in their cars in the church parking lot and listened to the service either broadcast or through open windows. Many utilized internet resources and either prerecorded a sermon and music that was then posted on the church's website or on social media websites like Facebook or YouTube or some even livestreamed a service that was conducted before an empty building where all the congregants could "check in" and say hello to one another and then occasionally hit a Like button instead of saying "amen." Still others, depending upon the state and directives they were under, held a number of mini services each Sunday so that the number of congregants that were at any one service remained under ten and could maintain a six-foot separation.

[60.] Emphasis added.

Irrespective of the methodology utilized, many pastors found ways to not live in fear of the government or have their congregants operate in fear as they came to worship by finding a new, if somewhat unusual, way to obey both the government and the Bible. I guess that is my point here. As long as the government does not demand that a Christian does something that is expressly prohibited or completely prevents them from doing something that is required, then an attitude of humility and an understanding that according to Romans 13:1 all those in authority are *instituted by God,* and we are to submit to them and their authority. The upside to all that is not only will we be obeying God's Word, but we also won't have to have any level of fear as to what the government will do to us.

OCTOBER

But you, son of man, do not be afraid of
them or their words, though briers and thorns
are beside you and you live among scorpions.
Don't be afraid of their words or be discouraged
by the look on their faces, for they are a rebellious
house. (Ezekiel 2:6)

My guess is that if you were to stroll into almost any church in
America and ask people when was the last time that they had read
or studied the book of Ezekiel, the numbers would be fairly small.
With its emphasis on prophecy that came through a series of visions
and the use of a lot of metaphorical imagery, many do not venture
into its pages other than to extract a verse or two. So let me put the
first verse for this month into context. The prophet Ezekiel is given
a vision that starts off with seeing the Lord's glory in chapter 1. As it
happens in Scripture almost every time, when God allows just a tiny
bit of His glory to be seen, the recipient goes to the ground because
they cannot stand in the presence of an indescribable and awesome
God. Chapter 1 closes with Ezekiel hearing God speak to him.

Now that Ezekiel knows how incredible God is, through His
Spirit, God brings him to his feet and begins to describe to Ezekiel
what he is to do, which is to speak for God and give God's people a warning due to their longstanding rebelliousness against God
and His law. So Ezekiel is to go before the leaders and people of his
country and tell them that God is going to deal with their consistent disobedience. God even warns him in verse 4 that He knows
that the people are *obstinate and hardhearted*. What a great assignment. People generally don't respond really well when you tell them

that they're messing up, and now the messenger knows going in that they're not going to be receptive. I suppose that would give anyone pause to go into a task like that without some level of apprehension. And that brings us to our first key passage this month.

During my police career, one of the most dreaded assignments is having to deliver a death notification. You never know what kind of situation you are about to encounter. Sometimes the news is expected, and the receiving party is grateful that you came to inform them. Many times, though, the information comes seemingly from out of nowhere, and the recipient is suddenly devastated, and you're left standing there trying to console a person whom you've never met before about a situation that has completely caught them unprepared and has devastated them. The younger the person who died is, the more likely that the second response would occur. To make matters worse, you often have virtually no information other than a person is dead and the people can contact whichever agency or detective put in the call for service. In a profession that prides itself on finding solutions to problems, you are suddenly absolutely impotent to help the very citizens that you have sworn to protect and serve. You politely ask if there's anything else that you can do for them, knowing that there's not, then turn and return to your patrol car as the grief pours from the doorway you just left. Rarely they may even attack you verbally or physically in their shock, but despite there usually not being any physical danger, the event has left you wishing that you hadn't come into work that night.

Ezekiel is given a much bigger notification to deliver and knows that it's not going to be well received, which had to really concern him, so God tells him twice in this one verse to not be afraid of doing what you have been tasked to do, even when you know going in that is not going to be pleasant. This passage is full of some figurative language, so if we are going to learn another aspect of avoiding fear, then we are going to need to understand what we are seeing here with the briars, thorns, and scorpions that Ezekiel is shown to be in the midst of as he fulfills his mission. Briars and thorns are seen as signifying rebellious and disobedient people who impeded your progress and can also cause some damage and pain as you try to pick your way through them. Of course, there are thorns, and then there are big thorns.

*   *   *   *   *

One night, I responded to a hot call of some people who were breaking into a car in a townhouse parking lot. As luck would have it, I was right around the corner and got on scene really quickly. The victim/caller contacted me and gave a good description of two girls and a guy and their last known direction of travel. I assured the victim that I would return shortly and headed out to see if I could find the suspects, and things worked out really well, and I found them casually walking down the road a few blocks away. I got out of my car and ordered all three of them to stop and sit on the curb. The two girls did, but the male decided to run for it. I knew that other officers were en route, so I went in foot pursuit. The suspect wasn't getting away from me, but I wasn't catching up to him either. To his chagrin, the road was a long U and was starting to turn back and head toward where we'd left his two female accomplices and my patrol car. So instead of heading back in that direction, he opted to try jumping over a residential fence and see if he could lose me that way. That's where he made his critical mistake (other than committing a crime and running of course).

Remember, it was nighttime, and that was a particularly dark one. You could see that there was a large bush in front of the home's wall, but he thought he'd just jump through it, boost himself over the wall, and escape. What he couldn't see in that near total darkness, though, was that this particular bush was a bougainvillea. If you are not familiar with this plant, at certain times of the year, some of their leaves take on some incredible color, and it looks like a huge collection of flowers. But the plant has a strong defense against would-be eaters, the stems boast strong thick thorns that, on a large mature plant, can be two to three inches long. The young man jumped into that bush and just stopped. He had impaled himself almost head to toe, and as I caught up to him, all I could hear was a rather soft moan and a plea to help remove him from his plight. When my backup officers arrived a few seconds later, we pulled him from his predicament, and it sounded a bit like when you pull Velcro apart. The paramedics arrived, but he had already stopped bleeding, so after a few bandages were applied, he got to spend the rest of his evening as a guest in the county jail. Now those are some serious thorns, but let's get back to Ezekiel and his potential thorn problem.

Like the young man whom I just told you about, Ezekiel was going to experience the irritation and pain that rebellious and disobedient people can bring into your life, especially when you are giving them God's Word that shines the light on their bad attitudes and behavior. But if that's not bad enough, God also points out that he's living among scorpions. Where I live, bark scorpions are a thing, particularly the closer you live to undeveloped areas of natural desert. According to the Mayo Clinic's website, this type of scorpion is the only scorpion species with venom potent enough to cause severe symptoms.[61] Great, but at least they're not one of the thirty species that have venom that can potentially be fatal. Also, for those of you who don't know, scorpions are an arachnid (like spiders—eight legs and jaws that go sideways), and you already have read about my problems with arachnids in all their manifestations. When you live in an area with scorpions, you learn to avoid doing certain things like moving things in the garage that have been sitting in the same place for a long time without seeing exactly where your hand is going to go. At night, particularly in the summer, when you may be barefoot, you pay attention to where you're placing your feet. Even though they are not out to get you, you also know that they are very aggressive with anything that comes within the grasp of their pinchers or tail stinger. So you remain cautious and try to make your home as uninviting as possible.

God reminded Ezekiel that the rebellious people that he lived among with had some very scorpion-like qualities. He didn't need to be afraid of that situation, but he did need to be mindful that they were there and of what harm they could potentially inflict. Then

---

[61.] Accessed June 12, 2020, https://www.mayoclinic.org/diseases-conditions/scorpion-stings/symptoms-causes/.

God told Ezekiel not to be afraid again, but this time it's not the external attacks characterized by briars, thorns, and scorpions. This time it was internal.

Most of us, I think, know this old rhyme: "Sticks and stones will break my bones, but words will never hurt me." If we ever get to that level of maturity and resiliency, we are doing incredibly well. For most of us, though, words can hurt us and often do. The hurt can range from a mere irritation or a sharp pain that is quickly removed (like pulling out a small sticker from your foot) to a severe wound that in some extreme cases can even lead to the fatality of the victim. Words do hurt. In God's second statement to Ezekiel about fear, He tells him to not "*be afraid of their words.*" In giving Ezekiel this command, God is letting him know that the people to whom he is bringing God's Word are not going to respond well and they're going to verbally respond in ways that are most likely going to be very painful to Ezekiel. It's fairly common in my experience that when someone doesn't like the message that you're telling them, they don't attack the message; they attack the messenger.

*   *   *   *   *

During my career in police work, I was called things that you don't even see scrawled on bathroom walls. My integrity was assaulted, and my actions were often attributed to hate, prejudice, or evil intent. None of that was true, and generally, I usually could shrug it off; but there were times, especially when I was trying to go above and beyond what I was required to do to help someone, that those verbal attacks would make it through my defenses. The pain they caused made me want to say "Okay, fine, you're on your own" and walk away. But thankfully, the more common response was to remember that they were hurting and stressed and lashing out and to just keep doing what I knew to be in everyone's long-term interest.

Who said to them, "Tell your master this,
'The LORD says: Don't be afraid because of the
words you have heard, which the king of Assyria's

attendants have blasphemed Me with.'" (Isaiah 37:6)

This verse about not being afraid because of words comes out of the middle of a story, so let me put it into context for you. Hezekiah was the current king of Judah. He's in the capital city of Jerusalem, and his country was being attacked by the major power of his time, King Sennacherib of Assyria. All the fortified cities in the kingdom had already fallen, and the army had come to Jerusalem. Instead of setting up a siege or just attacking the city, the king sent an emissary to propose a bloodless surrender. He let them know that for the time being, their normal life would go on until the king was ready to move them somewhere else where, ostensibly, they were to be a controlled workforce for the Assyrian nation. Hezekiah had sent out three officials of his court, and upon hearing what Sennacherib's minion had to say, they entered into complete despair and reported to Hezekiah what the terms were. Hezekiah also became completely dismayed and went to the temple to pray. While he was praying, he sent some of the same men who had received the terms of surrender to talk to Isaiah, whom they recognized as a prophet, and ask him to intervene for them with God. Without hesitation, Isaiah responded with a direct message from God by telling them to not be afraid because of what they had just heard because those words had actually been an attack on God Himself. In fact, the next verse, which continues God's message, God told them that King Sennacherib was going to hear some things himself and his reaction to what he heard would lead to his death: *"I am about to put a spirit in him and he will hear a rumor and return to his own land, where I will cause him to fall by the sword."* (Isaiah 37:7).

With the incredible growth of social media, people now hear things, as information gets shared and reposted over and over again. Few even bother to check the veracity of that information even though it may be only partially true or even just a downright falsehood. But the old adage "Repeat a lie often enough, it becomes the truth" takes hold and suddenly people believe it and often verbally attack anyone who disagrees with the so-called true idea. The problem is that many of these supposed truths, even if they are mostly or completely accurate, have been packaged in such a way as to elicit a response of fear to either get someone to spend money on a product, vote for or against something/someone, or do any other of a number of manipulated responses. Perhaps the most nefarious one is just to scare as many people as possible and then sit back and watch the mayhem that follows.

During my time on the police force, some of these internet rumors would come around from time to time, and invariably some of my friends and/or relatives would send them to me so that I would know. A few would ask me if I'd heard this information and if it was true. One of my favorites that came around several times was the notion that drivers were not to flash their headlights at any cars driving with no lights on. The message claimed that, as part of a gang initiation, gang members will chase any car that flashes them and shoot and kill all the car's occupants. I have never been able to establish that this has ever happened anywhere on the planet, but the shelf life of this rumor predates even social media. My limited research on this one indicated that it may have originated as far back as the 1980s with the Hell's Angels or some other motorcycle gang as the possible bogeyman, although I cannot confirm that to be true either.

Whatever the source or the intent of words are to scare us, they often do have a powerful way of accessing our most primal fears of losing everything that we hold most dear, starting with our life and health. Of course, for Hezekiah and his advisors, it wasn't a rumor. Their country's fortified cities had already been sacked, and the full force of the Assyrian military was sitting in the valleys outside of Jerusalem itself. The words they got from King Sennacherib's lackey was obviously true, and now they had an offer to avoid a military conflict and the fate of the other cities if they would just agree to be conquered. Fear ruled the day.

I love God's response here. Since Sennacherib had used words to try to instill fear and to insult God, God was going to use words to stop him and send him to his doom. What a great plot twist. In fact, later in the chapter (verses 33–34) God said that King Sennacherib and his army would not enter the city, build siege ramps against it, or even get close enough to shoot an arrow into the city. He would go back the way he came to his own country and capital of Nineveh (currently known as Mosul) in modern-day Iraq and die there. This kind of fear exposes the fact that on a primal level, we understand that we're not really in control of our lives. We like to think that we are, and most of us work really hard to try to be in complete control, but then something or someone comes along and strips away that veneer, leaving us to fear what is coming next. The only way that I've found to combat this type of fear is to know and rely on God who is in control of everything all the time.

Later in the book of Isaiah 43:13, we read this: "*I am God now and forever. No one can snatch you from me or stand in my way*" (Contemporary English Version). Now combine that statement of power with Romans 8:28, which reads, "*We know that all things work together for the good of those who love God: those who are called according to His purpose.*" How can I be afraid of anything that someone says or even does to me if both of those statements are true?

This kind of fear, for a Christian, is really a faith issue. Do I believe God is who He says He is? Do I believe that whatever happens, even if by the world's standards it's really awful or even fatal, is in my best interest? While I may hear things that rightly cause me to adjust my current course, it must not ever cause me to completely abandon what God has called me to do. Fear-generating words are just that, words. They have no power other than what I grant them to have. If I believe in what God's Word says, this kind of fear becomes a thing of the past.

Let's look at one more fear this month, regarding things that are spoken.

> When a prophet speaks in the LORD's name, and the message does not come true or is not fulfilled, that is a message the LORD has not spoken. The prophet has spoken it presumptuously. Do not be afraid of him. (Deuteronomy 18:22)

For a lot of people, a pastor or another religious leader holds a position that seems loftier than the rest of us mere mortals. Some of those leaders like to cite the story of Moses, Aaron, and Miriam from chapter 12 in the book of Numbers, particularly starting with the second half of verse 8 and continuing with verse 9, which reads, "*So why were you not afraid to speak against My servant Moses? The LORD's anger burned against them, and He left.*" If you don't know the story, Moses's older brother and sister were speaking ill of Moses and wanting to be on an equal plain with him as far as importance goes. God heard this and called all three of them outside of their tent and then came to them in a pillar of cloud and told Aaron and Miriam in no uncertain terms that it was Moses who was His chosen messenger and that to speak out against him was to question God. After He gave them that correction, He left, but Miriam was suddenly completely leprous. In fact, that debilitating skin condition that we now know as Hansen's disease was instantly in such an advanced state that she was described as "*white as snow.*"

While we should not be speaking against those in authority over us as a general rule, it's especially true for those who are our spiritual shepherds. There are a couple of problems that come out of this idea. Some religious leaders use this concept as a shield against any criticism or correction even when they are openly violating biblical precepts. The other problem is the opposite side of that same coin when church members think that they cannot approach a pastor or deacon who appears to be teaching false doctrine or becoming involved in activities that they should not. Faith traditions other than my own may also employ titles like prophet or apostle for some of their leaders, and based upon the various Bible stories, those titles may carry even more weight in people's minds. This means that the possibility of abusing this concept is even greater, and yet both the Old Testament and the New Testament require godly men and women to be judging what people who are speaking for God (Old Testament) or from God's Word (New Testament) are saying to see if it's accurate. Now I know a lot of people find the word *judging* to have too many negative implications, so let's go with *fruit inspecting* then. We are to be inspecting the fruit of what they're saying and doing, not just blindly following.

In this last verse for this month, God even sets up the standard for any would-be prophet. Their message has to come true or be fulfilled every time or they are not speaking for God. And so God says, "Don't be afraid of them." The word here is that same concept of respect and awe when we fear God himself. God says to not be afraid of what they are saying and to not give them the respect that is reserved for God and His word alone. Of course, the people who engage in this type of behavior don't want to be criticized or questioned. They want blind acceptance and usually lots and lots of money or power and control over others for their own aggrandizement. This kind of false prophet is always out there. Whether it be men like Jim Jones or any of the cadre of so-called faith healers who are bilking millions of dollars from people worldwide and grossly missing the 100-percent mark that God laid out. Any leader, though, who is up to no good or acting presumptuously can fall into this idea. In my department, most of the command staff were made up of really honorable men and women, but there were a few that you had to be careful around. They were careful to only give verbal directives, and then if something went wrong, they would distance themselves from the issue and deny having ever said something or adjusting it to the point that the original directive was almost unrecognizable.

*   *   *   *   *

In the 1990s, small pocket-sized mini cassette recorders that were voice-activated became very popular on my department. This was long before bodycams were invented, and having a recording of your conversations with the public often proved to be very beneficial both as a memory jog when you were writing a report and also as a defense mechanism when someone claimed that you had or hadn't said something. You can probably already see where this is going. Officers or sergeants would turn them on before meeting with their superior officer. The vast majority of the time, it didn't mean anything, but if you had one of those supervisors who liked to keep all their directives verbal and then obfuscate or deny if things went wrong, they suddenly found themselves unable to do so when the officer produced a taped recording of their discussion. Strangely enough, after a few supervisors had to eat their words and own up to their mistakes, we got new policies that forbid taping a superior officer unless they were aware of the taping. Did all taping of conversations with superiors stop? Hardly, but officers were much more discreet and would hold on to a taped meeting as an insurance policy just in case. I can tell you, though, that you didn't have to tell someone of a lower rank not to fear (respect and awe) the officer in the upper rank if they had pulled off this sort of shenanigans. But there was a reasonable fear that they might do it again, so some took measures to protect themselves. In case you're wondering, this never happened to me, as the recorder or the recordee, but I was aware of a number of cases.

While I don't advocate recording every conversation that you have with someone in authority, particularly in the church, I do encourage people to be fruit inspectors. Check out what they are preaching or teaching. Be like the people in Berea who, when Paul arrived in their town and started preaching the gospel, *"examined the Scriptures daily to see if these things were so"* (Acts 17:11b). If you will do that, not only will you get a lot more out of the sermon or teaching, but you'll also be able to rely on that leader more and more, and together you'll move a lot further in your Christian maturity than if you had just blindly followed and accepted. Plus, you won't suddenly find yourself in the midst of a bad situation, wondering how you got there and becoming bitter because a sinful person was acting exactly like a sinful person even though they carried some official title in the church.

Be a consistent fruit inspector and don't allow the false prophets that are seemingly everywhere these days and often apparently doing really well financially to sway you. God is completely just, and the day of reckoning is coming. James 3:1 says this: *"Not many should become teachers, my brothers, knowing that we will receive a stricter judgment."* While that verse doesn't keep me up at night, it does keep me on my toes to make sure that I'm biblically accurate in everything that I teach or write. I've read about God's judgment, and I can only imagine what a stricter judgment can mean. Instead, I'm shooting for Matthew 25:21—*"His master said to him, 'Well done, good and faithful servant! You were faithful over a few things; I will put you in charge of many things. Share your master's joy.'"* Notice that God doesn't say "Always perfect servant." His focus is not on perfection that I cannot attain. It's on being faithful, consistently obedient, and then dealing with sin when it crops up. When I'm doing that, then there is no fear of judgment, stricter or otherwise.

November

This month, I'm going to look at three additional words that are translated as fear and see what they mean so that we can identify them in our lives and work on not being afraid as Scripture repeatedly commands us not to be. Let's look at the first one.

> Damascus has grown feeble; She turns to flee, And fear has seized her. Anguish and sorrows have taken her like a woman in labor. (Jeremiah 49:24 NKJV)

The word translated as fear in the various King James versions, Webster's Bible Translation, and Young's Literal Translation among others, is the Hebrew word *retet*, which means to tremble or be in terror.[62] Other Bible translations do use the word *tremble* instead of *fear*, and a number of them translate the word to *terror*. In most modern translations, the word is translated to our English word *panic*. So with that information in hand, let's look at the verse in context and see what we can get out of it.

In Jeremiah chapter 49, the prophet is giving God's Word as to what is going to happen to a number of Judah's enemies, including Ammon and Edom, before He turns his attention to Damascus. Damascus (in modern-day Iran) is the capital of Aram or Syria and first came to prominence under Rezon sometime after David's death (1 Kings 11:23–24). Throughout 1 and 2 Kings, we find Damascus and the Syrians involved in almost constant wars against Israel and Judah or teaming up with Israel against Judah. The prophets

---

62. Strong's 7374.

147

Amos and Isaiah have already spoken out against this city, and now Jeremiah gives God's final word against it. Damascus was subsequently conquered by the Babylonians around 605 BC (which is probably what is talked about here) and then again by the Persians around 530 BC and again by Alexander the Great in 333 BC.[63] But as Mark Twain wrote in his 1869 work *Innocents Abroad*,[64] Damascus is "the oldest metropolis on Earth, the one city in all the world that has kept its name and held its place and looked serenely on while the Kingdoms and Empires of four thousand years have risen to life, enjoyed their little season of pride and pomp, and then vanished and been forgotten."

At the time of Jeremiah's prophecy, though, Damascus is relatively strong and a regional power, but her long-time harassment of God's people is about to come to a sudden end. Jeremiah points out that the city has become weak, which happens, and history is rife with example after example when a society becomes powerful and no longer fears being destroyed. Instead of standing to fight, her military forces turned to run. Terror and panic have taken over the hearts of the inhabitants who feel as though this has happened suddenly, like the onset of labor pains. This kind of fear implies that there is no longer any thought other than to get away. This is what is often referred to as a blind panic, the kind of mindless running that can be seen when a peaceful and unsuspecting crowd is suddenly attacked like the October 1, 2017, mass shooting in Las Vegas.

I have only seen this level of fear a few times in my life, and thankfully, at least so far, I have never experienced it. In each of the cases that I observed, there was thankfully no loss of life, but trying to stop a group of people whom have entered that level of fear is pretty much impossible. At best, all you can hope to do is channel their blind need to escape in the direction that you want them to go. But you better not get out in front and try to stop them. If you're lucky, they'll just go right past you. If not, they'll go over you. Either

---

[63] Accessed on June 16, 2020, https://www.lonelyplanet.com/syria/damascus/history.

[64] Currently available through CreateSpace Publishing at most major booksellers.

way, their natural fight-or-flight response has kicked in, and almost nothing is going to slow them down until it subsides. The result of this kind of fear and panicked fleeing means that there will be no resistance to the carnage. In fact, just two verses later, God, through Jeremiah, says, "*Therefore her young men shall fall in her streets, and all the men of war shall be cut off in that day*" (Jeremiah 49:26 NKJV). Whenever you turn your back to an enemy, you are no longer able to defend yourself. It can take an incredible act of the will to face what is coming at you when running seems like the best option. And when God says the word *all*, He always means it.

The urge to blindly run in the face of danger is a universal truth that even shows up in our humor, like the story of two friends hiking in the woods when they are suddenly confronted by a grizzly bear. As the bear is sizing up his upcoming meal and dessert, one of the hikers turns and begins running back down the trail as immediately does his friend with the bear now in hot pursuit. His friend asks him what he's doing and then points out that you can't outrun a hungry bear, to which he responds, "I know that. I just have to outrun you." So the question, then, is how, when you're suddenly confronted with a situation that is more likely than not to be fatal, to not succumb to the kind of panic-inspired terror that would cause you to just blindly run in the first direction that you see. How can you either stand and face the situation or make a reasoned retreat to a position of safety?

We have to know, and remember, what God says in verses like Isaiah 41:13, which says, "*For I, Yahweh your God, hold your right hand and say to you: Do not fear, I will help you.*" And Psalm 118:6, which reads, "*The LORD is for me; I will not be afraid. What can man do to me?*" Why would I be afraid of anything if God Himself is holding my hand? This kind of fearlessness, I think, is best personified in the story of David and Goliath from 1 Samuel 17. In this story, the Israelite army was facing the Philistine army with both sides camped on opposite hillsides. In keeping with the custom of the day, sometimes to avoid a lot of bloodshed, each side would select a champion to represent their side for single combat, with the losing side either surrendering or withdrawing after the battle. The problem for the Israelites was that the Philistines had a champion by the name of

Goliath who was a true giant. At nine feet, nine inches tall, he was already an imposing figure. But 1 Samuel goes on to describe him as being decked out in bronze armor from head to toe, with his armor alone weighing 125 pounds. The spear he carried was so big that the iron spear point weighed fifteen pounds. In case all that wasn't enough, he also had a shield bearer whose sole job was to walk in front of Goliath and carry a shield big enough to protect him.[65] Both sides are at a standoff because no one in the Israelite army, under their very first king Saul, is willing to answer Goliath's daily challenge to end the conflict with a champion-versus-champion battle. Three of David's older brothers have been enlisted into the army, so their father sends David with some provisions for them and to check on their welfare. He witnesses the two armies lining up in their battle formations, and then Goliath comes out for his daily challenge, and according to 1 Sam. 17:24, the Israelite army retreated in terror.

David is incensed at the audacity of Goliath to stand up to the Israelites and can't understand why no one would go down and take him out. Eventually he makes the offer to King Saul to fight Goliath, but Saul recognizes that he is but a youth. (Most commentators have him, based upon the Hebrew word used here, in his mid to late teens.) And yet eventually he relents, and without the benefit of armor, David goes to face Goliath. Here is where the story gets especially interesting. David, armed only with a sling, grabs five smooth stones and goes to face the giant. But why five stones? Was it so that he could reload as necessary? Probably not because Goliath had four brothers (see 2 Samuel 21:16–22 and 1 Chronicles 20:6–8). David understood the custom of the time that if you killed someone's family member, then the family would come to avenge them. David was prepared to take out the entire family with one stone each. Talk about confidence! But you see later that he is the one who wrote Psalm 118. He was a true believer that there was nothing that man could do to him without God's permission and that this Philistine was defying God. This made him not just fearless but also confident

---

[65.] See all of the above descriptions in 1 Samuel 17:4–7.

that he would defeat Goliath with a single stone and then take out the rest of his family if necessary.

The Bible points out that David did run, but it wasn't in abject terror and panic like his three oldest brothers and the rest of the Israelite army. 1 Samuel 17: 48 tells us that after a verbal exchange with Goliath as to what they were going to do to each other, David ran *at* the armored giant and his shield bearer, not away from him. With one single stone, David drops the giant and then uses Goliath's own sword to kill him and decapitate him. The battle was over before it even began.

* * * * *

People often asked me throughout my career if I was afraid. I had to honestly reply that there were a few moments here and there, but for the most part, Psalm 118:6 and Isaiah 41:13 gave me the assurance that I could run to the danger and not away from it. Now let's look at another word for fear.

> The fear of man is a snare, but the one who
> trusts in the LORD is protected. (Proverbs 29:25)

The Hebrew word here translated as fear is *chărâdâh*, which means to be so anxious that you quake or tremble.[66] This sort of fear is best illustrated by one of my dogs, Amy Rose. I have two golden retrievers (Jane and Zelda) and a much smaller Boston bull terrier named Amy. She is really terrified of fireworks and gunshots. So on the Fourth of July and New Year's Eve, as soon as the first firecrackers go off in our neighborhood, Amy is in my lap and literally vibrating as she trembles with fear that somehow those loud noises are signaling an upcoming monstrous attack on small Boston bull terriers everywhere. No amount of cuddling can abate this reaction, although she is usually very willing to be held for the rest of the evening, so I often find myself holding a vibrating dog for a long time. That is the kind

---

[66] Strong's 2731.

of fear this word means in this verse, so let me paraphrase it for you and insert that meaning because then it would read like this: "Being so afraid of others that you are quaking is a trap, but a person who trusts in the Lord is completely protected."

It is possible for someone to become so afraid of what others are saying or doing that they begin to hyperventilate and to just quiver in place and unable to move or think clearly. When you are hyperventilating, you are breathing out an excessive amount of carbon dioxide, so your body responds by slowing the blood supply to a number of areas. This can leave someone with a tingling or numbness sensation and the inability to move. My friends working for the fire department have told me that this is a very real thing. They have had to physically remove people from situations who had just frozen in place. Of course, this was from a fire or some other physical disaster, but you get the picture. Sometimes, though, this type of quaking fear doesn't inhibit our physical movement, but it traps us in other ways. For a Christian, it often exposes a lack of trust in God's promises and care. We can become so freaked out by what others are saying or doing that we become ensnared in the sense that our thinking and actions are either reined in or completely controlled by the person or group that we are so afraid of. A quick look at history will show you that a small minority who is extremely vocal and engaging in some violent and destructive behavior can effectively control a much larger group, as individuals within the larger group are too afraid to become a target, so they just comply and either limit or change their behaviors. Eventually the trap-induced change can become so thorough that a person's thinking begins to change as well, and over time, the new or limited behaviors are seen as normal and correct.

The verse lets us know that trusting in the Lord doesn't just let us avoid the snare, but it also puts a person into a place of safety. In a number of translations, the verse closes with either the phrase "set on high" or "kept safe." The Hebrew word that we get "protected," or "kept safe," or "set on high" is *sâgab*,[67] and it means essentially that you are put up so high (exalted) that people can't get to you. You are

---

[67.] Strong's 7682.

so secure in Him that no amount of intimidation or even physical assault can make it up to the place that God has put you. Now that's a protected place.

The military, in relation to ground wars, is always looking to occupy the high ground because an enemy that has to attack you is at an extreme disadvantage. They have to overcome not only the change in elevation but also your own defenses and counterattacks. Taking out a well-entrenched position on the top of a hill can be virtually almost impossible. A great example is when a small number of Jews (around one thousand, including women and children) held off the approximately fifteen-thousand-man Roman army at the mountain fortress of Masada for almost two years. That's the advantage of being put up in a high place.

Isn't it great to read that when you trust in the Lord, He puts you into such a lofty position that no one can get to you? Why, then, would any believer in the Lord God choose to be afraid of what someone is saying or doing? To do so is to deny that you occupy such a high place that people, with either their words or actions, can never successfully get to you. This kind of fear is based on this physical world being the end-all and be-all of a person's life, that what happens here and the pain or pleasure that you know is all you can ever experience. If that was true, then God's Word isn't true and you are not in a protected high place at all. In fact, things can go so horribly wrong that you're left quaking and unable to think or move.

As a society, we really seek to celebrate those individuals that overcome what, for most of us, would be this kind of fear. In the military, the highest recognition of this kind of fearlessness is the Medal of Honor, which is given to "those who have distinguished themselves in actual combat at risk of life beyond the call of duty."[68] For my former department, a similar award is the Medal of Valor, which is "awarded to an employee for a conspicuous act of valor during the

[68.] Congressional Medal of Honor Society, accessed June 25, 2020, www.cmohs. org.

actual performance of a police service that involves the risk of life and knowledge of that risk."[69]

One recipient of that medal was Officer William "Bill" D. Cheatham. He responded to a call of a suicidal individual, and as he arrived at the person's home, he observed the man getting into his car with a brown paper bag, and Bill knew that the caller had stated that the subject was armed with a handgun. As the subject drove away, Bill began to follow him while deciding what would be the best course of action to keep everyone out of harm's way. Within a few minutes, two other marked units joined Bill, but the subject was not driving erratically or breaking any traffic laws, so they just continued to follow him in a slow pursuit that predated the famous O. J. Simpson bronco event by six years. Suddenly the driver stopped in the midst of a residential street. Bill stopped, and when he saw the driver's door open and the driver starting to exit, Bill stepped out of his car and drew his service revolver. Before he could even address the driver, though, the subject had fired his .44 magnum, and incredibly it missed the car and the door frame and found its mark in Bill's right shoulder. Now I know in movies and TV Westerns, a mere shoulder wound allows the hero to stay in the fight and defeat the bad guy. In reality, though, it usually takes you right out of the fight. Bill later described it to me as like being hit with a fastball from a major league pitcher except that instead of a baseball, it was a bowling ball."

The force of the impact knocked Bill to the ground and made his right arm useless. As the subject started exchanging gunfire with the other two responding officers, Bill got back up, used his left hand to retrieve his service revolver from his dangling right arm, and returned fire one-handed, with his unsupported left hand striking the subject in the chest and ending the threat. I asked Bill how he had the wherewithal to get back into the fight after taking that kind of damage, and he simply told me that he was too afraid not to because he thought that the subject might come around his car and "finish me off." Still, this was an incredible act of bravery that was properly

---

69 Accessed June 25, 2020, https://www.phoenix.gov/policesite/Documents/ Program_2017_Master_PPD. pdf#search=police%20medals.

recognized for what it was: something that most people couldn't or wouldn't be able to do.

Most of us recognize that these exceptional acts that are recognized by the Medal of Honor or the Medal of Valor are way beyond what a normal reaction would be. And yet, according to Proverbs 29:25, this is the level of fearlessness that should be normal for a Christian. When we are physically or emotionally attacked and our weapons of survival are dangling useless by our side, God says that our actual position is one of protection that is so lofty that no one can get to us. You see, God is looking at the situation from the perspective of eternity. We, on the other hand, are looking at the problem from the right now. When we learn to trust in what God says about us, then instead of sitting on the ground quaking that they are going to come finish us off, we can get back up and face the attack because we know that they can't get harm the part of us that is eternal. God has the believer protected.

Let's look at one more word for fear this month. We'll go back to the book of Isaiah.

> And it shall come to pass in the day that the LORD shall give thee rest from thy sorrow, and from thy fear, and from the hard bondage wherein thou wast made to serve. (Isaiah 14:3 KJV)

The word translated as fear here is *rôgez*[70] and has the meaning of a commotion, restlessness, crash, disquiet, or anger. The visualization is of a horse that is worked up and crashing about his stall. The root word it comes from has to do with any violent emotion including fear. So this is a fairly powerful word. Subsequent to the King James quote above, modern translators use the words *suffering*, *turmoil*, or *torment* when they translate this word. Use the word picture of the horse, though, stomping about and kicking at his stall

---

70 Strong's 7267.

because something has him so emotionally worked up and read the passage again.

To put this verse back into its context, Isaiah is writing to the Israelites who are going to soon be taken into captivity by Babylon and removed from their homes and homeland. Here in chapter 14, God is telling them about the eventual fall of the king of Babylon and the song of deliverance that they will eventually be able to sing. But He knows that after their years of captivity that as a nation, they are going to be like that horse that is really upset with his confinement in a stall. They are afraid that they will never be restored and be a free people again, and God tells them that He is going to give them rest from their state of restlessness as they crash about against the bondage of the Babylonians and their fear that it's never going to end.

Have you ever felt like that? You feel trapped and confined, and you're afraid that it's never going to end. It may be a job issue or a medical problem or something else that has you convinced that this is your new normal. Fear can convince you that whatever you're currently experiencing is never going to end, and that can make you really restless and cause you to stomp and kick at whatever stall that you're standing in at the moment. More than anything else, this kind of fear or turmoil prevents you from seeing that there are many other possibilities and, if left unchecked, can lead to despair and severe depression and all the negative physical and/or emotional things that depression can bring into your life.

Most of us have probably run into someone who has become trapped in their despair. They have become perpetual Eeyores (the always down and depressed donkey from the *Winnie the Pooh* stories by A. A. Milne). They have moved past the stomping and restlessness of a trapped animal and have succumbed to a depressed position of just being, a person who has no apparent hope that anything will ever be different or better than their lot in life. This is always bad, but it's even worse when the person is a believer. Uncontrolled and continual fear can show up in some really harmful ways. Medical science tells us that it weakens our immune system and can cause cardiovascular damage and gastrointestinal problems like ulcers and irritable bowel syndrome. It can even lead to decreased fertility, accelerated aging, and even premature death. The mental damage is even worse.

As I've studied fear, I've learned that it can impair the formation of long-term memories and cause damage to certain parts of the brain, which then makes it difficult to regulate additional fear. To a person living in chronic fear, the world looks like a scary place, and their memories confirm that. But not only memories are affected; fear can mess with the processes in our brains that allow us to regulate our emotions or to read nonverbal cues and to react to information without reflecting or acting unethically. And then finally, things like fatigue, clinical depression, and even PTSD can set in. When we succumb to fear over a long period, we can move from the restless horse kicking around his stall to one who just listlessly stands in the corner waiting for the next bad thing that we know is going to happen. I have never met someone, at least so far, who has moved to this state of being almost catatonic because of constantly living in fear, but I have met several who resemble the kicking and stomping horse.

In the 1980s, I was a supervisor for the Best Western hotel chain, working out of the main reservation center. At one point, the decision was made to open a satellite reservation center in the women's prison that was located at the time in an old hotel in central Phoenix. The idea was to train a number of these women so that they could learn a marketable skill (for when they were released) and to allow them to earn a much better wage than the prison paid for minor work around the grounds so that they could begin to pay off their restitution (if they had any) for their crime. For a young twenty-something, moving into this world was a complete shock. The prison housed low-, moderate-, and high-security women, but the company only employed mostly low-security and a few nonviolent moderate-security inmates. As I interacted with my employees, I got to know a number of them and their stories. A lot of them were mothers who were now separated from usually very young children because of their crime and were anxious to be reunited because they didn't know how their children were doing. Some even had not been visited by their child either because the child was too young or because their guardian (usually a family member) refused to bring them. The women in that last category were afraid that either their child (or children) wouldn't remember them, wouldn't have a relationship with them, or were not being raised well or were even being abused. Those women were like that proverbial horse. They were constantly kicking about their "stall" as fear about their children's welfare gripped them. They saw working for Best Western as a way to both escape just thinking about the situation with their children and as a means to hasten their release date by showing good behavior and a responsible work ethic.

In getting back to the verse, though, there is an answer for this kind of fear-based torment and worry. The verse says that the Lord gives rest. That word *rest* means to settle down, which is the perfect complementary word picture to our restless horse kicking and stomping around its stall. But of even greater significance is that this is a promise to God's people, not a general promise to all mankind. Looking at the verse in its historical context, this statement is looking to the end of the Israelite captivity in Babylon. The promise comes into effect after the people have lived through the judgment that was meted out to them for not obeying God in the first place. God is promising to restore His people and bring them home, which will allow them to settle down from the worry and stress that they experienced in captivity.

I cannot even begin to recount all the times that I have experienced something similar. Too many times I've found myself worrying about things that I cannot control and the fear that ensues that causes me to become unsettled and to stomp and kick at things around me in my frustration. It's not until I give up trying to figure it out myself and give it to God that He grants me the rest that I'm looking for. When He does, then and only then do I become settled in my thinking. My stomping and kicking about return to calm, and my fear fades to nothingness.

December

Well, we've come to the last month of the year. So far, we've looked at a lot of different kinds of fear and how they are addressed. Back in the introduction to this book, I told you that my intent was to help you know that fear of any created thing or situation should not be the controlling aspect to a believer's life and to show what a healthy fear (or correct concept) of God should be and what it looks like. So I'll finish with three more words that are translated into fear, knowing full well that I've only scratched the surface on everything that God's Word has to say on the subject. I wanted to end on somewhat of an upbeat note even though we're talking about fear, which generally is decidedly anything but upbeat. So let's examine those last three words and concepts, and I'll try to finish in a positive vein.

> For I hear the slander of many; Fear is on every side; While they take counsel together against me, They scheme to take away my life. (Psalms 31:13 NKJV)

Being talked about negatively and slandered is a really big fear of many, particularly in this time of social media where faceless, and often nameless, people seem to live for the opportunity to destroy others through their words and opinions on everything, from what someone is wearing to whom they vote for. When it becomes severe, this particular kind of fear even has a name; it is called anthropophobia, which is the extreme, irrational, and unwarranted fear of people or society.[71] According to the website FearOf.net, in its most virulent

---

[71.] Accessed July 17, 2020, https://www.fearof.net/.

state, this fear can cause people to try to avoid social events, feel panic when meeting people, and have a constant thought that they are going to embarrass themselves in some form or fashion. While most of us probably will never get to that level, many of us have likely felt the sting of having been talked about in a very unflattering way by other people.

The Hebrew word that is translated fear in this verse is *mâgôwr*[72] and is often translated in other Bible translations with the word *terror*. King David is the author of this psalm, and he feels the terror of being gossiped about by a lot of people can bring, especially when it gets to the point that people are beginning to figure out a way to kill you. Now in David's life, there were several times when this was true. The most egregious of these times was when one of his own sons, Absalom, plotted to take away his throne.

I am hoping that most of you will never experience the level of being slandered and plotted against like David did, but my guess is that a number of you are already thinking about a time when you experienced something like it. It could have been at work, school, church, or even in your own family; and when it happens, it not only hurt, but it also may have made you really afraid to ever venture out into public again. And what's even worse is that you usually don't even know about it until it's too late. Of course, this kind of attack isn't relegated to just personal affronts, as businesses face the same kind of issue, and if you're a small business owner, you most likely know just how devastating negative opinions posted in various online formats can be. This is such a problem that there are now businesses whose sole mission is to defend or repair online reputations because of the very real fear of being destroyed by some anonymous person seeking to do your business harm. So far, I can gratefully report that this has never happened to me, at least not that I'm aware of. And yet that fear that it can happen is like a lot of other fears; it lives just at the edge of my peripheral vision. I find myself wondering what people are thinking and saying about me after my most recent sermon or Sunday school lesson. Even as I write about this fear, I have to

---

[72.] Strong's 4032.

confess that thoughts of what people might say about me because of this book have crept into my head from time to time. So like most of us, you can see that my favorite person to think about is me.

In verse 11 of that same psalm, David described what had happened to him because of this pervasive gossip: "*I am ridiculed by all my adversaries and even by my neighbors. I am dreaded by my acquaintances; those who see me in the street run from me.*" He experienced some very real consequences of others talking about him. Being ridiculed by your adversaries is to be expected to some degree, although you'd rather be respected by them. But when your neighbors join in based on what they've heard and your friends start finding ways to avoid you, then you know that the damage can be very real. Essentially, this kind of an attack is a theft of a person's reputation. The real problem lies in the fact that for all the recipients, those who've heard the gossip and drawn a conclusion about someone, is that there is usually no way of knowing just what is an outright lie, what is sort of accurate, and what—if anything—is actually true. So you can see how David would find that to be terrifying. One minute, you're the highly respected king of Israel, and then almost suddenly, you find that your friends won't talk to you and your neighbors go in their house and shut their door when you come out of your house. It can feel like everyone is out to kill you off, if just in the metaphorical sense. If you want to read about an especially egregious example of this, look up the story of Robert and Iwona Woch and how a simple horse-drawn sleigh accident led to the destruction of their reputations.[73]

The Bible says in Proverbs 18:21 that "*life and death are in the power of the tongue.*" We get a lot of our concept of who we are from our community. We try to notice how other people are responding to us and what they are saying to us, specifically what they say to us about us. The impressions that we pick up from other people by what they say can be life-encouraging to us or they can be life-exhausting. So when your reputation is stolen, you can feel like you've had your

---

[73] You can find the complete story at https://www.buzzfeed.com/alanwhite/how-a-fake-story-ruined-three-peoples-lives.

life sucked away. Our next word translated as fear is going to address this fear or terror and give us the confidence to go on despite what others may say about us.

> The fear of man is a snare, but the one who
> trusts in the LORD is protected. (Proverbs 29:25)

The word for fear here is the Hebrew word *chărâdâh*[74] again, and remember, it has the idea of extreme quaking or trembling. What this verse is saying, though, is that when we get so afraid of what others are thinking or saying about us that we're shaking inside that it can lead to us making some really foolish and sinful decisions to try to alleviate that fear. Sin is often described as a snare, and the best example is Proverbs 5:22, which says, *"A wicked man's iniquities entrap him; he is entangled in the ropes of his own sin."* This is exactly what most of our reactions tend to be when we're gossiped about or outright slandered. We either go on the attack in the hopes that we can make the issue go away or we pull away and just try to avoid people altogether. The problem with both those reactions, though, is that they are sinful because they directly violate what Jesus described in Matthew 22:39 as the second of the two greatest commandments: to *love your neighbor as yourself.*

For those of you who don't know, the biblical idea of love has very little to do with feelings and a whole lot to do with actions. Love is about what we do, not how we feel, because feelings can be very fickle from one minute to the next. Love is therefore a choice. You choose to love others by doing things for them. And as Christians, we are to love others like Jesus loved us, which is sacrificially and without first establishing the merit of the person to be loved. This is what Jesus did for us; He loved us when we weren't lovable. We did nothing to deserve His love, and yet He paid the penalty for all our sins. That is the ultimate love action. So if we're to love others like that, then either the response of attack or withdraw is missing the mark of what God says we are supposed to be doing. You can't be

---

74 . Strong's 2731.

loving your neighbor if you're attacking him or avoiding him. You'll end up getting caught in the snare of your own sin. All too often, the final result of either wrong choice is that not only do you still have some level of the same fear, but the problem has become even worse.

During my career, I often had one of my peers who would come to me and complain about how they felt that they had been mistreated by their supervisor. Generally, the response wasn't to attack but avoidance by transferring to a different squad, precinct, or specialty assignment, even if that transfer was less desirable than what they had. My counsel was usually to tell them to stay put if they liked their current assignment and if it worked for their family. The reason for that is that people regularly moved about the department, and the chances were that they could transfer into either a worse situation or that they would transfer and then so would the supervisor, so they would have disrupted their lives for nothing. I also told them to figure out what their supervisor liked and then really excel in that aspect of the job. So yep, I was encouraging them to love on the supervisor they didn't like.

Almost everyone I've ever talked to has a story or two about a boss that they didn't get along with for one reason or another. I had bosses that were easier to get along with than others, but I learned rather quickly that if I followed the second of the two greatest commandments that while we might never be friends, I could basically get along with them, and after a while, they tended to leave me alone as long as I wasn't making any glaring errors. And that leads me into the second half of our verse for this section, which is the antidote for both the aspects of fear that we've examined in this month: "*The one who trusts the Lord is protected.*"

To trust is to have full confidence in and to act accordingly. This is faith in action, but it's not blind faith. This is trusting in the God of creation. This is having faith in the God who is described in the book of Job as literally giving us our next breath (Job 34:14–15). The proverb promises those who have that faith that they will be protected. That word *protected* or what many translations have as *safe* means to be set on high. I've already given you that picture earlier, but here it is again. God says that if you'll have actionable faith in Him, He will put you in a place where other people can't really hurt you. Now does that mean that you'll suddenly go around being invulnerable or that people will just leave you alone? Nope, but it does mean that they can't harm the eternal and permanent you. Jesus pointed this out in Matthew 10:28 when He said, "*Don't fear those who kill the body but are not able to kill the soul; rather, fear Him who is able to destroy both soul and body in hell.*"

You see, the Bible points out rather consistently that as a Christian, "*you will have suffering in this world*" (John 16:33). This is true because we are no better than our Lord Jesus, so if He suffered in this world, then we can expect to as well. But the next phrase from this verse is where the encouragement comes in: "*Be courageous! I have conquered the world!*" That's the protection, that's the safety, and that's the high place that He promises to put us in which is within the throne room of the one who has already conquered the world. So why, then, would I be shaking and quivering about what other people are saying about me or doing to me? Why would I try to go and fix the situation in ways that violate God's commandment to love my neighbor, especially knowing that God says that it's going to be a trap that catches me instead of dealing with the person who is trying to hurt me? That just would be foolish.

Okay, I said that I would end on a positive note, and knowing that God will put me in a high place is pretty positive as far as I'm concerned. But let me finish the book with one more word that's translated as fear in English. And since I can only think on one thing at a time, I can't concentrate on fear and something else, so let's go back to the book of Psalms one last time and find something else to do with our minds instead of being afraid.

> You who fear the LORD, praise him! All
> you descendants of Jacob, honor him! Revere
> him, all you descendants of Israel! (Psalms 22:23
> NIV)

The last Hebrew word for fear that I'm going to look at is *yârê,*[75] and it has to do with awe-inspired reverence. This is another Davidic psalm that starts out with David crying out to God because of his suffering. Then in verse 21, David suddenly shifts his tone when he says, "*You have answered me!*" (NKJV). Knowing that God has heard him in his distress, David praises God for His goodness and mercy. David explains why he is so joyful in verse 24: "*For He has not despised or detested the torment of the afflicted. He did not hide His face from him but listened when he cried to Him for help.*" David acknowledges that God knew about his problems and answered when David earnestly brought those problems before Him. David believes that he was not only serving a God of magnificence and power but also a God who knew and cared about him as an individual. Because of this, David calls on everyone who has awe-inspired reverence for God to engage in three concepts in worship: praise him, honor him, and revere him. David starts out with praising from which both honoring and revering will flow. The word *praise* here is *hâlal*[76] (the root of *hallelujah*), meaning "to praise, honor, or commend." There is an implied attitude of thankfulness that precedes and is encompassed in the praise. The word also carries the idea of expressing admiration for something or someone that is worthy to receive it because of what they have done. This worship is done to God.

Then David calls on God's people (*"All you descendants of Jacob"*) to honor Him. To honor someone means that you give a positive public proclamation about the other person. So David is calling on everyone who fears the Lord and is engaged in thanking Him for who He is and what He's done to, then publicly proclaim how awesome God is and how He hears when His people call on Him. Wouldn't it be incredible if everyone in the world today who names Jesus as Lord would boldly and publicly tell anyone and everyone about the positive attributes of God? Perhaps it could just start out with the fact that He knows you by name. He knows what you're going through

---

75. Strong's 3373.
76. Strong's 1984.

right now, and He answers you when you call on Him. This worship is done about God.

Finally, David calls on God's people to revere Him. This is the Hebrew word *gûwr*,[77] and it has the idea of turning off the road and staying at a place for a while. The old word that isn't used anymore is *to sojourn*. So to continue David's train of thought here, because God knows His people individually and their circumstances and hears them when they call out to him, then they should praise and thank God directly, tell others about how wonderful their God is and all His positive traits, and then finally, they should stay in this place for a while. Worship isn't to be a drive-by or something that is done in 140 characters or less. It's to be a place that we stay in and offer praise and honor. For most of us, this is difficult. We are so easily distracted, and there is always something that is coming at us. Often it's something we didn't anticipate or prepare for, and so now our focus shifts from our awesome God who knows what we're facing to the problem itself. We see the storm and not the God who controls it. We forget the promise that we see in Isaiah 41:10 where He tells us that He is with us and that He will strengthen us, help us, and hold on to us with His righteous right hand.

This is the best kind of fear, to be so awestruck that the awesome and indescribably powerful God, who spoke the universe into existence, knows and cares about you as an individual. But there's good news and bad news here. The bad news is that all the promises that we've looked at throughout this book are only for God's people. The good news is that God is constantly calling new people into His forever family. And now for the best news: all you have to do is to accept Jesus as Lord of your life to be a recipient of them. You do that by believing that He lived a sinless life, physically died, and then physically rose to life three days later. Then according to Romans 10:9, the only thing you have to do is tell someone about it. That gets back to the honoring thing that I talked about earlier. In my experience, this isn't a have-to; it's a want-to because when all the weight of your cumulative sins is suddenly gone and you're in touch

---

[77.] Strong's 1481.

with the God of creation who knows you by name, you want to tell anyone who'll listen.

I'll leave you with the words of God to His people through the prophet Isaiah in Isaiah 41:10: "*Do not fear, for I am with you; do not be afraid, for I am your God. I will strengthen you; I will help you; I will hold on to you with My righteous right hand.*" May your fear only be positive reverence for God and not all the others that we have looked at over these twelve months.

About the Author

Harry and his wife of forty years are professed desert rats, as their families have lived in the deserts of Arizona since the territorial days. They have five children and eight grandchildren (so far) spread around the country. He served with the Phoenix Police Department from 1990 through 2017, having served in a number of assignments. He received his Master of Divinity, with a specialty in chaplaincy from Liberty University and, upon his retirement, became a chaplain for the Phoenix Police Department and a professor teaching administration of justice courses in the local community college district. In 2019, he also became a part-time associate pastor of his church.